Resilience and Self Esteem For Women

Dr. Barbara Becker Holstein

Contents

Introduction IX

1. EMBRACE OPTIMISM DAILY 1

2. LIVING A MISERABLE LIFE 3

3. DESIGN YOUR HAPPINESS 5

4. BREAKING THE GLASS CEILING 9

5. CREATING SUCCESS 13

6. FINDING THE ENCHANTED SELF 15

7. PERSONAL TRUTH IN CREATIVITY 17

8. COPING VIA POSITIVE MEMORIES 19

9. FINDING JOY 21

10. SWEETHEARTS 23

11. REDISCOVERING ANNE FRANK 25

12. PRACTICING GRATITUDE 29

13. FINDING HAPPINESS IN AGING 31

14. USING FANTASY 35

15. MENTORING 37

16. CONNECTING 43

17. PERSISTING 47

18. CARING ENOUGH 49

19. BEING KIND 51

20. CULTIVATING LASTING HAPPINESS 53

21. FINDING ENCHANTMENT IN WISDOM 55

22. SAVORING ENCHANTING MOMENTS 59

23. FINDING BLISS 61

24. SAVORING LIFE 63

25. HAVING BEST FRIENDS 67

26. FINDING THE ENCHANTRESS WITHIN
PART 1 69

27. FINDING THE ENCHANTRESS WITHIN
PART 2 73

28. DELIGHTING IN OURSELVES 75

29. DARING TO GO BEYOND OURSELVES 77

30. BUILDING SELF-ESTEEM, PART 1 81

31. BUILDING SELF-ESTEEM, PART 2 85

32. FINDING HOLIDAY MAGIC 91

33.	SELFIES AND SELF-ESTEEM	93
34.	THE POWER OF SELFIES	95
35.	RETRIEVING POSITIVE MEMORIES	97
36.	FLYING HORSES	101
37.	WOULD YOU INVITE ANTS TO YOUR PIC-NIC?	105
38.	GOING BEYOND LOSS	109
39.	OWNING OUR PASSIONS	115
40.	MEETING OUR NEEDS	117
41.	POSITIVE PSYCHOLOGY FOR WOMEN ONLY	119
42.	FINDING MIDLIFE ENCHANTMENT	125
43.	FINDING YOUR ENCHANTED SELF	129
44.	DREAMING	131
45.	RESTORING YOURSELF AGAIN AND AGAIN	135
46.	REMEMBERING THE BEST	139
47.	HONORING OUR TRUE PASSIONS	143
48.	FINDING BLESSINGS	145
49.	TAKING EASY STEPS TO ENCHANTMENT	147

50. NANCY DREW AND YOU AND THE TRUTH — 151

51. SELF ESTEEM THROUGH MEMORY — 153

52. PRACTICING GRATITUDE — 155

53. FINDING PLEASANT MEMORIES — 157

54. NEW YEAR'S RESOLUTIONS — 161

55. OUR SPECIAL ANGELS — 163

56. HAVING FUN — 167

57. FINDING A TREASURE CHEST — 169

58. DESIGNING YOUR LIFE — 173

59. FINDING MAGIC POTIONS — 177

60. CHILDREN AND SELF ESTEEM — 181

61. CREATING A MENTAL PLAYDATE — 185

62. KIDS HAVE DEEP THOUGHTS AND FEELINGS TOO — 187

63. And finally — 191

64. Building Resilience and Self-esteem: Interview with Moumita Basuroychowdhury, Part 1 — 193

65. Building Resilience and Self-esteem: Interview with Moumita Basuroychowdhury, Part 2 — 199

66. Building Resilience and Self-esteem: Interview   205
with Moumita Basuroychowdhury, Part 3

Introduction

I'm hoping you look at and enjoy this book as if it were a delicious box of chocolates or another treat you look forward to. Think of it as a new friend in your life, always available, not picky or annoying, just there to provide a taste of pleasure and advice whenever those aspects of life might come in handy. Treat it like a poetry book you could open to any page and get a lift out of it or a treat.

My first Positive Psychology book: *The Enchanted Self: A Positive Therapy* is set up chapter by chapter with many exercises you can do yourself to move closer to your Enchanted Self. It is a beautiful book, and I advise reading it if you haven't.

Now comes the dessert: this book. Any page you put your finger on and read can be interesting and will touch upon some aspect of being a woman in today's world. There is a lot of wisdom and advice in this book. Enjoy taking that wisdom and advice into your life as you play with getting closer to your own Enchanted Self. That's where your wisdom and delight in bringing to life your true potential lies.

Let me know about your Enchanted Self journey by writing to me at barbara.holstein@gmail.com. I'm hoping my next book can be a compilation of your story alongside many other women's stories as you move toward being an Enchanted Self.

Chapter One

EMBRACE OPTIMISM DAILY

This quote is from Alexandra Stoddard's book, *Gracious Living in a New World*.

"One day of optimism is a start. A day can be a microcosm, a tiny representation of all our days, of our whole life. There is no reason why the lessons of our one positive day could not stand for what we need each and every day of our lives, as a family and for ourselves."

This is a great quote and true. It is never too late or too early to practice optimism. I teach that in THE ENCHANTED SELF® and the little girl in my book, *The Truth: I'm Ten, I'm Smart and I Know Everything* knows it also. Maybe she knows it intuitively, as perhaps most of us did before we became "grown-ups." The little girl knows how to practice being in a great mood by riding her bike down hills and letting the wind blow her hair back. And she knows how to think good thoughts before she gets out of bed in the morning— imagining nice things that can happen.

Chapter Two

LIVING A MISERABLE LIFE

You know that I usually talk about the secrets to living a great life. After all, I am a positive psychologist and originator of THE ENCHANTED SELF. But I'll talk negatively also, if I think I have a chance at convincing my audience to look at life from a more positive vantage point. So, here are my 7 Secrets to Living a Miserable Life:

1. Constantly put yourself down.
2. Worry, worry, worry.
3. Dwell on every little thing that has gone wrong in your life.
4. Focus on your weaknesses.
5. Think that your future will be as lousy as your past.
6. Practice being in a bad mood.
7. View yourself as nothing special.

Let me know what you think of this list, and trust me, I have the cure for the above complaints!

Chapter Three

DESIGN YOUR HAPPINESS

As many of you know, I am a positive psychologist and happiness coach—I encourage finding out what's good about ourselves (rather than what's bad) and seeing ourselves in a positive light. I teach how to understand your own needs and your talents, and how to do the work necessary to create a life full of happiness.

I'd like to share with you a happiness process I developed from many years of observation, case studies, and happiness research.

In my happiness research, I found that women are happy at least part of the time, but often dismiss their good feelings as just a blip on the "radar screen of life." They also frequently lose their "good mood" as soon as someone criticizes or puts them down.

I began to realize that becoming and staying happy requires a habit that can be practiced and improved upon. I developed a model called THE ENCHANTED SELF that shows how we can improve our happiness using something I call "Recipes for Enchantment."

def. THE ENCHANTED SELF — the capacity to initiate positive states of being unique to our disposition and talents.

def. Recipes for Enchantment — the ways we've found to create happiness for ourselves that are unique to us.

The Enchanted Self is something you control, and you do it using "Recipes for Enchantment" that are unique to you.

Although there are many "Recipes for Enchantment" that most of us have in common, it's important to remember you are unique, and what makes you happy isn't necessarily going to be the same for the other people in your life. YOU are the "secret ingredient" in the recipe for creating your own happiness. As such, you must discover the unique things that enhance your happiness.

Here's a "recipe" for discovering some of the unique things that make you happy...

Exercise: Recipe for Personal Pleasure

Give yourself a quiet space, a pad of paper and a pen, and permission to daydream. The world is your oyster. Plan out a day that is designed to make you happy.

– What would that day be like, and what would you do?

– Where would you go?

– Who would be with you, if anyone?

– What would you see?

– How would you feel?

– What would you eat that day?

– What are some of the aromas that would please you that day?

– What would be the highlight of the day?

– How would you feel at the end of the day?

Now you're looking back on that day.

– What would you be most pleased about?

– What are some ingredients you would need to make this day come true?

– What could be three steps YOU need to take to get closer to experiencing a pleasing time right now? [Remember YOU are the main ingredient.]

Chapter Four

BREAKING THE GLASS CEILING

When I was a little girl, many moments uplifted me. One of them was moving from New Haven to Bridgeport at the age of five. At first, I was very sad because the man in the moving van had strapped my red two-wheeler bike to the back of the truck, and I was afraid it would fall off as we drove to our new home. My dad assured me it would not fall off, and I saw the strong ropes holding it. I was happy, because my dad had just taught me how to ride that bike after many times running alongside me up and down the street as I learned how to balance on a bike. I couldn't wait to ride it again once we got to Bridgeport.

But what I didn't expect happened on one of the first days I attended Elias Howe School. It was a holiday of some sort. They told us kids it was May Day, and there was a May Day pole with long ribbons all around it. We got to hold a ribbon and run around the maypole. Somehow, this moment in Bridgeport has stayed in my mind all my life as the first time I really felt I was an American. That school, with limited funds and almost no books, so old we had to hold fire drills all the time and run down the metal stairs, made me an American with all the depth a five- or six-year-old can take in. That's where I learned about Betsy Ross sewing the flag and other stories about George Washington, whose picture hung in each classroom.

Over the years, my feelings of being an American have run very deep, also influenced by my grandmother Rose Silverman who would sit me on her lap as we sat on the front porch and sing "God Bless America." That song, I'm sure, meant a lot to her because her parents immigrated to this country, her mother at the age of four, and her father when he was about 11. Both had left behind war torn areas of Europe not partial to Jews. America was a dream come true for my great-grandfather, Isaac Watchmaker. After selling rags and eating boiled eggs for years as he tried to make a living as salesman of rags, pots and pans, he became a wealthy man. That's a long rags-to-riches story that symbolized the American dream. That it was my family's story, made me an American who could also rise.

But I was a woman not a man, so what did that mean to me? Luckily, my dad was a visionary who saw the ways that women could come into their own talents. He pushed me to get my doctorate before I had kids, as I'd be less tired at that point in my life. How right he was. And yes, I walked out of Boston University with a doctorate in Education and a well done thesis on creativity in children.

But then life took me and my husband and baby to New Jersey where we lost easy ties to family and friends. I learned, as millions of women learn, that feeling fulfilled as a woman is a personal journey of many years. I found my path through becoming a psychologist and recognizing that I had two incredible traits: one was from my dad. Not only that, I was also a visionary who soon realized that psychologists had missed the boat in much of the treatment they were offering. Simply put, it is just as important to help people develop their talents, interests, and potential as it is to help them solve their problems.

Helping people develop their potential has become my life's work. What my mother gave me was my ability to share in words, through writing or speaking, about what needed to be said.

As a woman, I still realized that there was a glass ceiling. I might or might not break through. I now believe that the ceiling is really made out of plastic. We can break through and are breaking through more and more often. Brilliant women such as Kamala Harris are showing us the way by their actions and their words. I'm so proud to be an American, I want to dance! I'm imagining myself in the arms of George Washington, and here comes Abraham Lincoln to ask me for the next dance, and here comes Kamala Harris to pull me aside to introduce me to Bill Clinton and Rosa Parks or Margaret Thatcher.

Got to run now. Lots to still do and be, and I want to be part of it. Thank you, Elias Howe School for getting me filled to the brim with being an American.

Chapter Five

CREATING SUCCESS

Continuous effort - not strength or intelligence - is the key to unlocking our potential. ~Winston Churchill

Simply put, this is a great recipe for success. My father always said that inspiration was 99% perspiration and 1 % inspiration. It is the persistence and the capacity to hang in when our ideas, our dreams, our talents — even our style or way of being — are not easily accepted that makes us stronger and eventually starts to turn the tide.

Positive Psychology comes into the mix in that we have a chance as psychologists to help people understand the true nature of success — that it is a process not just a given, and to help people hang in to see themselves in a positive light and not to give up. This is not easy. It requires training and perspective. I train using THE ENCHANTED SELF model, helping people to reclaim their earlier talents, strengths, interests, coping skills, and even hidden or lost potential. I combine the training with a healthy dose of hope and optimism. It is a good recipe!

Chapter Six

FINDING THE ENCHANTED SELF

Today, I was going through some old papers I have collected around THE ENCHANTED SELF. My initial positive memory work and the resultant shift for the treatment room actually happened years ago. In fact, I wrote the rough draft of *The Enchanted Self: A Positive Therapy* at least 30 years ago, before the movement of Positive Psychology was given its name. When I put up my first website, THE ENCHANTED SELF, in 1996, I did not use the term Positive Psychology, as it was not "coined." Instead, I talked about the disease model in psychology and the need for a shift in the treatment to help clients use their memories to retrieve and celebrate what was right about themselves instead of what was wrong. I talked about rediscovering our talents, our lost potential and bringing positive states of being back into our lives. I talked about courage and hope and also the need for therapists to go on the same journey as their clients since we, too, get depleted, discouraged and even forget what is best about ourselves.

The only thing I didn't talk about was Positive Psychology! How ironic, as I am indeed a passionate Positive Psychologist.

Anyway, I was pleased to find in a pile of papers a remark made by Helen. I'm sorry, I don't remember who Helen was. She said, "Memories are the embroidery of our lives. Those are heirlooms you are making!"

Chapter Seven

PERSONAL TRUTH IN CREATIVITY

I was with my two grandchildren, and the four-year-old girl was singing a song. Her brother, age six, said to her, "Stop singing that song!"

She said, of course, "No, I want to sing this song."

He said, "It's not real. You made it up."

She said, "It is real, I made it up, and I am singing it."

What a human dilemma. My husband and I sided with our granddaughter that indeed it was real. Even if only one person knows the song, she has every right to sing.

Our grandson was stuck in the notion that you call a song something that many people know and acknowledge as a song. After all, no one else could ever sing the song if she forgot it!

Wow! Where does THE TRUTH lie? In my book, *The Truth: I'm Ten, I'm Smart and I Know Everything*, the girl has a song that only she knows. It becomes very important to her as she gets older. And it is a problem that only she knows the song! I will keep a little mystery around what happens.

So, what do you think? What makes something real?

Chapter Eight

COPING VIA POSITIVE MEMORIES

Many of my readers write to me about the tensions of everyday life. Not only do people wonder how to relax, but people often ask, "How do I learn to better cope with what faces me? Can THE ENCHANTED SELF help with the overwhelming frenzy of everyday life? Can it help when I am down or when something really goes wrong?" Absolutely!

In my newsletter, I often talk about the power of our positive memories. I emphasize this power because so often people focus on their negative and unpleasant memories. However, THE ENCHANTED SELF is much more than the retrieval of positive memories. It is the recognition of what works to make us thrive as human beings and the courage to live fully. One of the marvelous ways we can use our enchanted memory banks is to look backwards in time to recognize our coping skills......

What are some of your coping skills? Congratulate yourself for having and using them!

Chapter Nine

FINDING JOY

The Rebbe Nachman of Breslow often said, "Remember: Joy is not merely incidental to your spiritual quest. It is vital."

As the years have gone by, and I've been in the practice of psychology many years, I have become more and more convinced that he was so right. Joy is not an option. When we take away joy, and we take away a sense of well-being, a sense that we are thriving, we allow ourselves or seem to find ourselves in circumstances that drain, tire and weaken us. We are no longer the whole human being that is our birthright!

THE ENCHANTED SELF is a positive psychological approach to mental health that works both in the treatment room and out. I teach people the techniques they need to start so they can think in positive ways about themselves and their world. Thus, I teach them how to see what is right about themselves, rather than what is wrong. I also teach them to appreciate their own life story, its ups and downs; the roller coaster ride that we all go on. I teach how to value our potential even if in childhood we were put down or criticized, as so many of us are.

Chapter Ten

SWEETHEARTS

There is a saying going around that goes something like this: On the day you were born, you were given a sweetheart for the rest of your life. Do you know who it is? It is you!

This sums up a profound truth. Of course, we are all hopeful and desirous of a special partner in our lives and many other people to love over a lifetime. But the truth is we need to be able to nourish, nurture, and enjoy ourselves. If we don't, we will not be in condition for the adventures, efforts, and commitments involved in joining up with others. Also, if we don't like ourselves, why would someone else like us? Think about these things as you take more interest in recognizing your own special talents, interests, coping skills, and untapped potential! Have fun getting to know a very special person.

Chapter Eleven

REDISCOVERING ANNE FRANK

More than 50 years have passed since Anne Frank kept her diary while in hiding! What a contrast to the freedom that most of us live in. I am fascinated by girl's diaries. Obviously, as my latest book is a girl's diary, *The Truth, I'm Ten, I'm Smart and I Know Everything*. I'm sharing with you my review of Anne Frank's diary. Have you read Anne Frank since you became a grown-up? If not, it is well worth a re-read. If you are younger than a grown-up, I'd love to know how her diary strikes you, living in today's world. Hoping to hear from you, so we can continue to talk!

The last time I really read the diary of Anne Frank, I was nine, in Sunday school in Connecticut, and pretty miserable. I had my own issues — some of the girls made fun of me, I couldn't learn to read Hebrew (no one had recognized that I had a learning disability), and I wanted nothing more than to really belong. Anne's diary made me cry and feel even more miserable.

This time, I'm a grown-up. In fact, my kids are grown. I'm a psychologist in private practice, with an emphasis on Positive Psychology. That means I encourage hope and optimism in my clients. I help them look for their talents and lost potential. And I just wrote a book in diary form, written by a 10- to 11-year-old girl, to help girls and their moms get in touch with the best of themselves. So, things are very different.

My reaction to reading Anne Frank this time was as if I had blinders taken away from my eyes. Instead of just seeing a girl in hiding and feeling oppressed with the sadness of her unfulfilled life, I saw a profoundly real teenage girl with unbelievable wisdom and honesty. She seems to be the compilation of all the inner knowledge, wisdom, sexual and emotional development of all girls. She is almost like the western world's Shakespeare for girls. For example, as a psychologist and a woman who was once a teenager, I was enthralled with her intimate feelings and thoughts around her crush on Peter. Lots of girls fall in love or have a crush, but few know how to process their feelings. In fact, that is why "the girl" in my new book, *The Truth*, falls in love: to help kids learn how to share these sorts of feelings. Anne understood so much about the ego development of a person in transition from child to woman. What she is able to put into words about her crush should help any girl experiencing deep and complex feelings.

I think every woman should take some time and re-read Anne Frank. You will certainly fall in love with her differently than the first time around. You may find yourself sobbing later, as I found myself, when her love of life and feelings and insights about growing up welled up inside me with the realization that Anne never got a chance to do all the things that most of us women take for granted: the husband, the kids, the first apartment, friends over, pets, just getting out in the fresh air!

Anne held on to her ideals and dreams, and she hoped that there would be a time that she could carry them out. She didn't make it, but we have. And so, if every woman who reads this book can just be a little more insightful, a little more caring, a little more loving, listen a little harder to kids and teens, then, in a way, we have carried out, as best we can, her ideals. As a positive psychologist and woman, this is my opinion of how to maintain hope and fulfill not only her potential, but our own.

Chapter Twelve

PRACTICING GRATITUDE

A few days ago, I lost my sense of smell. Suddenly, in the middle of a violent head cold it was gone. I realized that not only was I miserable, but I couldn't smell a thing, not even Vicks® VapoRub. Some of that was good news. Wow, the kitty litter box seemed so clean; no aroma at all. But that news grew cold as I reminded myself that I couldn't even smell pleasant odors. Over the next two days, I was keenly aware of the loss. I thought a lot about how important my sense of smell has been all these years. It had been my best friend many times, uplifting my mood by so many aromas: every spring when certain fragrances such as honeysuckle return, cinnamon, peppermint, fresh grass, chicken soup, musk perfumes, clean hair, even sweat. Panic almost began to set in. I needed my sense of smell. I was not ready to say goodbye. It became more precious by the moment. I resisted picking up the lavender soup to see if I still couldn't smell.

Fast forward — my sense of smell is back! Oh, sweet relief. I am leaning over my chicken soup — still simmering — and I can smell it again. I am still stuffed, but I am in wondrous awe of the trickle of aroma making its way through my passages. Not only that, but I realize I am in the *now*. I am in love with the smell of chicken soup. I am in love with my bathroom soap. Not only that, but I am in love with kitty litter. Well, not really in love, but appreciative.

The moment is passing. But I can say that I am so thankful. This is what feeling grateful really feels like. Not making a list when I wake up in the morning; nice idea but not passionate enough for me. This is pure gratitude, coming from the return of the most primitive sense we have, the one that is the gateway to so many of our memories. I love you. I love you. I love you. Stay with me forever. I will treat you (my ability to smell) with respect and awe. I promise.

Meanwhile, life goes on. I guess I have to change the kitty litter.

Chapter Thirteen

FINDING HAPPINESS IN AGING

People usually think late life is far from the best stage of life, but research in the *American Sociological Review* said the happiest Americans are the oldest.

This eye-opening research was conducted by Yang Yang, a University of Chicago sociologist. "The good news is that with age comes happiness." Yang said, "Life gets better in one's perception as one ages."

People in old age face a certain number of inevitable distresses, including aches and pains and the deaths of loved ones and friends. But older people generally have learned to be more content with what they have than younger adults, Yang said.

"Partly because older people have learned to lower their expectations, and they accept their achievements," said Duke University aging expert Linda George. "It's fine that I was a schoolteacher and not a Nobel Prize winner."

Yang's findings are based on periodic face-to-face interviews with a nationally representative sample of Americans from 1972 to 2004. About 28,000 people aged 18 to 88 took part.

There were ups and downs in overall happiness levels during the study, generally corresponding with good and bad economic times. But at every stage, older Americans are the happier ones.

In general, the odds of being happy increase 5% with every 10 years of age.

This is fascinating research. In general, I agree with the above conclusions posted in *China View*. As a positive psychologist, I believe that it takes practice to be contented with one's life and to experience a sense of well-being that didn't involve fame, fortune, or a body without cellulite. Of course, there is a good chance that older people get more chances at practice. Certainly, they have been alive longer! What I find is that there comes a time in most people's lives that they begin to relax into what the universe seems to have dished out to them. If they perceive this serving of life as basically a glass half full, they feel good about themselves and experience good feelings which are often interpreted as "happiness." If they see their serving of life as lousy, they often see the glass as half empty and miss many pleasant opportunities. Here is where practice comes in.

I am older, and I have intentionally been practicing being in the *now*, seeing the glass as half full. I can tell you it is worth doing! The other day, I went outside and not only hugged the tree on my front lawn but let it hug me with its two lowest branches. And then we rocked slightly in a very light wind. I can tell you it was pure pleasure. I could feel the energy of life in that tree. And I could feel the contentment build as we moved slowing together. It was an incredible few moments. And then I went inside, happy and content and loved, at least for the moment, by a tree.

Chapter Fourteen

USING FANTASY

Fantasy is a genre of fiction that uses magic and other supernatural phenomena as a primary element of play, theme, or setting. Many works within the genre take place in imaginary worlds where magic is common.

Often the genre of fantasy is dominated by its medievalist form, as can be seen or read in *The Lord of the Rings* books by J. R. Tolkien. Fantasy comprises works by many writers, artists, filmmakers, and musicians, from ancient myths and legends to many recent works embraced by a wide audience today. While fantasy art and recently fantasy films have been increasingly popular, it is fantasy literature which has always been the genre's primary medium. Fantasy role-playing games cross several media. The "pen & paper" role-playing game DUNGEONS & DRAGONS® was the first and is the most successful and influential, and the science fantasy role-playing game series FINAL FANTASY® has been an icon of the console role-playing game genre.

With the advancement of technology, more online communities have grown with role-playing opportunities. These websites attract millions of users worldwide ranging in various ages. What is it that attracts people of all ages to be glued to their screens for hours at a time? Are we starting to see a significant shift in behavior from people who spend much time in these fantasy worlds?

What attracts people to staying in these worlds for so long? When people are in online communities for hours what is being neglected in real life? What tools are available to users who may have difficulty distinguishing between fantasy and reality? The question may come up: is fantasy such a bad thing?

To better answer these questions, one may need an understanding of what makes us enchanted. THE ENCHANTED SELF shows us that many times we lean to a place that is removed from our reality. But what if we can turn the pleasure that we find in the world of fantasy into becoming part of our reality? To find out more visit www.enchantedself.com. Although not every fantasy has to have a Prince Charming, it can still be just as special.

Chapter Fifteen

MENTORING

Mentoring and learning from each other is much more than taking a course or explicitly giving someone advice or help. In almost every moment of every day, when we are with people, there is the potential for mentoring or a learning situation. We talk, gesture, and involve ourselves in many ways with many people. The exchange can be uplifting, informative, reassuring and kind, or it can be depressing, depleting, annoying, bothersome and more! I'm sure you can think of both good and bad times with other people!

I teach that experiencing THE ENCHANTED SELF is unique to each person. We all have our unique ways of feeling comfortable with ourselves, when we know that our mind, body, heart, and spirit are all lined up! We know that we are in stride with ourselves and our purpose in life for that moment. There is another level of Enchantment that we do reach, though, and this cannot be done alone. It is the shared positive experience of enchantment.

Can you even imagine what our world be like if everyone learned to tap into their Enchanted Selves often and while they were with others? I think the world would be more positive; a place where people would communicate in a friendly manner, respectful of one another's uniqueness and feelings.

Let's bring our discussion back to times we have all experienced. Haven't you encountered people who exude confidence and a sense of well-being? I bet you left the encounter feeling happier and more positive. Perhaps the next person you met had the opportunity to catch some of that positive energy. The truth is we all catch each other's moods and reactions. People often talk about how a smile brings on a smile. When we connect with our Enchanted Self, the joy and confidence we feel spreads to others. It becomes important to learn how to bring our positive states of being to the surface in such a way that others are encouraged to join in.

Certainly, we all respond better to enthusiasm and praise than disparaging comments and criticisms. Unfortunately, most of us are already experts on negative thinking and harmful criticism. Being in a good mood and then finding oneself in a negative situation is a difficult spot to be in. How quickly a positive state of mind can be interrupted!

For instance, we may be in a wonderful mood only to enter the workplace or home and be met by a scowl, a frown, or negative remark from a coworker or family member. How quickly one's positive state of well-being can dissipate. For example, if I walk into the house in a good mood and my mother, or my wife or my husband, immediately barrages me with a list of things that I didn't take care of or criticizes me for chores I didn't accomplish to their satisfaction, I will find the experience to be a clear interruption of my positive state of being. However, if someone were to gently say, "Can you give me a few minutes? I want to go over some of the chores we had agreed to split," or "I want to check with you as to what has been done or what has not been done," then I may be able to maintain not only my state of well-being but be in a good enough mood to help improve the other person.

A speaker once compared giving constructive criticism to that of a sandwich. The first slice of bread is telling the person something honest and positive about that person. The filling consists of gently leading into a suggestion or sharing one's feelings about how something is being done. The second slice of bread again finishes with a positive reaction or remark to that person. How desperately most of us need to practice the art of positive criticism.

Learning to communicate effectively to maintain each other's integrity and self-esteem goes a long way toward creating and spreading positive, productive energy and making the world a better place!

Exercise 1: Successfully Connect with Others

This is a very simple communication exercise that requires the consent and cooperation of a partner. Begin with allowing the other person to talk about something important to him or her for at least three minutes. The topic can be anything: their opinions about a complicated subject; their expert knowledge in some field; an anecdote about something that happened in the past; or their personal feelings about something or someone. After you have listened, give back only positive feedback. This is not easy, as we often find it easier to be an "expert" in criticism. However, it greatly enhances our mood to receive positive feedback. Reverse roles and allow yourself to talk uninterrupted for three minutes. Now, it is your turn for positive feedback. I can guarantee it feels better than criticism. Try it. You'll like it!

Exercise 2: Enhancing the Human "Touch" of Communication

Pick a day and have the fun of creating a special meal with family or friends. Carefully set the table. You could even put a flower vase in the middle or use a cloth table covering. Perhaps you could also start the meal with each person giving a blessing or stating a positive feeling about being together. Stretch and be generous of spirit — maybe you could invite the neighbor that would never expect to be included. During the meal tell positive stories about the "old" days or share funny stories about growing up. The immediacy of this type of human "touch" can turn an ordinary day into an enchanted one.

Chapter Sixteen

CONNECTING

I have a desire to share with you a beautiful story told to me by a young lady.

It was the end of World War II, and her dad was returning home. He came from a very close network of Italian families that lived near each other in New Jersey.

He had a ride back from where his ship had docked. Of course, he was filled with emotion as he came closer and closer to home. Suddenly, about five miles from home, he asked to be dropped off. He had decided to walk the last few miles himself and give himself time to emotionally "arrive."

He wanted to savor every moment of coming home! This was a time to feel the essence of the town he came from, to savor pleasant memories of growing up as he walked, and to allow his anticipation to build even further. Every step took him closer to friends and loved ones! He looked at every tree. He enjoyed every house he passed. He didn't even feel the weight of his duffel bag flung over his shoulder. He took his time walking. His parents knew that he was coming home soon, but they didn't know exactly when. Thank God he was alive! That knowledge was enough to sustain them.

Meanwhile, as he walked, several people recognized him. Some called out hello and several ran up to him and hugged him. He was offered rides but refused. However, behind closed doors the magic began. As he passed by these people, the news was quickly transmitted on the telephone that he was coming! Joe's son was home from the war. Pass the word. And they did.

By the time he got down to his street, several hundred friends and family filled the street as they waited for him. People shouted and clapped. He was hugged and kissed. Someone in the crowd took his bag from him. Everyone wanted to be near him.

"Make room for Joe and Rosie! For goodness' sake, let them get near their own son!" someone shouted.

He literally had to work his way through the crowd of neighbors and other relatives to fall into the arms of his mom and dad. How good it felt to be held again by the two people who loved him so much! And where was that pretty young woman that he meant to look up now that he was home? Oh, well, that would have to wait at least one more day. The rest of today was filled with fresh Italian foods, wine, hugs, stories and a place to come home to.

What a beautiful story. We all need a place to come home to — a place to be loved, to feel connected and with purpose. In THE ENCHANTED SELF, I teach about belonging and how important it is. I even feel the energy of this young man's connection to his people, and I wasn't there. The positive energy was so strong that it not only filled his granddaughter — but it could still be transmitted to me — and I hope to you.

He needed them and they needed him. He needed his time to re-enter. The energies connecting him with his tribe were so strong that he could not just be dropped off. He had to re-enter slowly at first and prepare himself for the intensity of connection. His tribe, likewise, prepared itself by a wonderful signal system — smoke coming up in puffs on the desert. The system worked so well that by the time he arrived a celebration was already up and running.

Tribes, or our special groups, are our gift to ourselves. They offer us a gateway so we can come back again and again. They offer us a signal system so that the important things are transmitted in a timely fashion, and they offer us the welcoming arms that help us belong, feel appreciated, and have a place. May each of us have the gift of belonging!

Chapter Seventeen

PERSISTING

Sometimes kids and adults forget how much resilience and persistence we can really muster. Life is not always easy, but we can grow as if we never give up. I was so lucky. I had a great mentor in my father. Many years have passed since he died on a May 16th. So, in memory of my dad, and with the hope of further inspiring all of you, here is one of the stories Dad loved to tell, even when he was gravely ill and in the hospital.

When my father went to camp at age 12, he was voted: the laziest, the least deserving, and the least likely to succeed.

Perhaps this was because he was tall and placed with boys several years older than he. Ironically, he was probably the least lazy, the most deserving, and one of the most successful people I have ever known. My dad was a loving husband, a loving father, and certainly a loving son. Beyond these roles and all of his connections with others, I believe he was an encourager of the human spirit. He was a realist who truly saw untapped potential in everyone who crossed his path — even me!

I remember him saying that persistence and perspiration would help me meet my goals. He loved to explain that most accomplishments are, "Ninety-nine percent perspiration and one percent inspiration." For example, when I was a teenager, he would help me wake up at 5:00 AM if I had homework to finish.

"Take a shower, have something to eat and then get back to task."

He was always there to ease my burden but not take it away. My responsibilities were my own to meet, not his. How could he be helpful but not do my job. Proofreading? Driving me to school late? Brainstorming a topic? He never, however, did work for me — it was mine to do. Like all good teachers, he never promised that he could remove my pain. He taught me that I could live with pain and get beyond it.

He was always my teacher. He taught me how to polish my shoes and to count my packages as I shopped, so I would know how many things I had with me. Above all, he taught me determination. Never give up. You can do it!

Chapter Eighteen

CARING ENOUGH

I will never forget how moved I was listening to Steve Hartman on CBS News. He did one of his "Everyone Has a Story" segments, and this lady certainly did. He had gone somewhere in Wisconsin, randomly found a lady and talked to her. At first, she tried to beg off and actually told him that he was violating her privacy, but after they talked for an hour, she shared a story that she had never told anyone.

About ten years ago, after her mother had just died and her husband had suddenly walked out on her, she was feeling very low. In fact, she kept thinking about a bottle of pills in her bathroom that she wanted to swallow all at once. She felt so terrible that she walked toward the bathroom to do just that when suddenly the phone rang.

It was an uncle of hers, just checking in, to see how she was doing. She lied, talked awhile, and then got off the phone ... to continue to walk toward the bathroom. The phone rang again. This time it was another relative, calling out of the blue, to see how she was doing. Again, she lied, and when she finally got off the phone, she walked down the hall toward the bathroom. Unbelievably, the phone rang a third time. Now, it was a friend from high school who hadn't called in years, just checking in.

Well, this time, when she hung up, she didn't go back toward the bathroom. She told Steve that never, never did she get three calls that close in a row; the phone sometimes didn't ring for days. She realized that these calls were somehow meant to keep her alive. In fact, she felt that the last caller had saved her life. She never attempted to take her life again.

Steve than went and found the woman who made the third phone call. He asked her if she was aware that she saved her friend's life. She was totally unaware and just barely remembered calling to say hello.

This true story, told for the first time, is incredible. Not only does it suggest the hand of the great Divine, but it also teaches us that we must act. Even the great Divine needs our assistance! We must act in each other's best interests. We must take the time to check in, to say hello, to see how each other is doing. We never know how much power the simplest gesture may have on someone else.

Chapter Nineteen

BEING KIND

Here's my story — at least the one that comes to me. I was in a play when I was eight. I had a walk on part, as a child in *A Streetcar Named Desire*, performed at the local college. The director, Mr. Dickenson, (Can you believe I remember his name?) sent me flowers and a note thanking me for being in the show and doing a great job. I must have read that note a hundred times!

How hard was it for an eight-year-old to play being an eight-year-old and walk across the stage holding a lady's hand? But he thought my acting was worth noting. Do you know how good I felt? How many times I read that note and memorized it? How special he made me feel? No wonder I remember his name. Thank you, Mr. Dickenson!

Let's all try to reach out — not only do we all have our stories, but we can all wave such wonderful magic wands for each other!

Chapter Twenty

CULTIVATING LASTING HAPPINESS

A happy woman is content in her life. She feels much peace of mind and a healthy level of enthusiasm as she goes through her day. Of course, she can become upset or angry, just like anyone else. But her happy nature works to her benefit, and soon enough she will find a way to return to a pleasant state of being that we call "happy," for lack of a more perfect word.

How is this so? Is she from a different planet than the rest of us women? Certainly not. She simply has learned and practiced many behaviors that help regenerate a state of happiness again and again. These behaviors that are practiced may include such common everyday things as eating healthfully and getting enough sleep. Also included are good habits around exercise and health care. Mentally, she has developed good social habits that make her fun and delightful to be with. This in turn means that she has lots of friends and doesn't feel isolated. Other behaviors carefully thought out and practiced led to her relating to her husband and children in a productive, loving way. In return, they give her the warmth and love that increase her happiness.

Of course, a woman may come up against very difficult situations and her happiness will be tested. A bad marriage or an ill family member, for example, may lead to situations that certainly don't feel "happy." But her capacity to make the most out of life, not by luck, but by utilizing good decision-making practices and other forms of resourcefulness, will lead her back on to a path of happiness. Yes, she may complain a bit during hard times, but not as much as a woman who is not practicing these skill sets. She simply won't have the time to complain, even during the down periods of life.

I can go on and on. But I think I have made my point. A happy woman has worked hard to get to her happiness and works hard to maintain it. It is well worth the effort. So, the lesson here is to work hard at upgrading all of our skills that increase happiness in daily living, both for the good days and the hard days. Thus, we can hopefully each say, "The harder I work at practicing happiness behaviors, the less complaining I do."

Chapter Twenty-One

FINDING ENCHANTMENT IN WISDOM

A while ago, I attended a beautiful wedding. A young Jewish couple came together in joy, and the room was filled with happiness. Outside the banquet room, I noticed a group of older women sitting near the door collecting charity. They all looked very pure and plain at the same time, young seniors and older seniors, nothing fancy about them. Their hips were full. They wore comfortable walking shoes and somewhat frumpy looking clothing. They wore either wigs or kerchiefs. They had a sweetness that if I were a child again, I would have felt delighted to have come home to milk and cookies with any of them. I ended up giving a dollar to just about each woman, in fact two dollars to the woman who actually changed a twenty for me so I could give out my money.

Later on in the evening, I went back out where they were, when nothing much was happening in the social hall, looking to have a bit of conversation with one of the ladies. I think I felt a need to be connected to their warmth. I certainly couldn't ask for milk and cookies, but I could chat with them!

The woman I spoke with was well up in years. She had beautiful, lively eyes; eyes that could have gone with a twenty-year-old or even an infant, they were so bright and full of life. Her skin was beautiful. Her body and her face showed age, but nowhere near the age that she apparently was. She told me that she came to this country 65 years ago with three children and went on to have seven more. That means that she is about 90. She didn't look a day past 75!

She told me that she comes out to all the weddings to collect charity. She's very proud of the fact that last year she collected $30,000 for poor, sick people in Israel and brides who needed money for their wedding expenses. She told me that she doesn't keep a dime for herself and that her daughter who lives in Israel helps to disburse the money.

By her intensity, I could see that she took her job extremely seriously and with utter devotion. She told me a few other things about herself. Her husband is no longer alive. She receives Social Security. Of her ten children, nine are living; one daughter was lost at 41 — I don't know to what illness. She is very proud that a number of her children are rabbis, teachers, and school principals in the Jewish educational world. That's about the extent of the details.

She opened a window to me. I never really knew, nor had I ever really talked to, any of these women asking for money at weddings. I guess, like we often do with people we don't know, I basically dismissed them almost as non-entities, even though I always gave at least a few dollars.

Talking to this woman made her so alive and real to me, as she obviously was for 90 years before I knew her! I was impressed with her generosity of spirit, her sincerity, and her utter devotion to her cause. She was passionately committed to her cause. She refreshed me with her energy and focus.

She is a woman, of course, who has known so many people and seen so many things! Having nine living children, she probably has 80 grandchildren. Her world is rich with people, children, and grandchildren and probably great-grandchildren to love. She lives a private life. Her name, even if I shared it with you, would not ring a bell. Her charitable work is not a registered charity. She doesn't go on TV with commercial pitches. She just comes to one wedding after another, sits out in the hallways, puts a little sign asking for money for the poor, ill, and brides in a dish and collects. Then she ships the money to Israel and starts all over again. There's no middle management.

There are no commissions to pay. There are no cuts. It's just dollar bills transforming lives.

It's simple. It's without layers. Lives are transformed without a middleman. This is the antithesis, the absolute opposite of the concept of managed care where one hand doesn't wash the other; where one hand may watch the other and takes a cut until there is less and less left.

Yes, as a positive psychologist and a woman, talking to her was really the best part of my week! She uplifted me and reminded me small is not less!

I hope you enjoyed my little story. Remember, the Seventh Gateway to ENCHANTMENT is Positive Action — Good Deeds!

Chapter Twenty-Two

SAVORING ENCHANTING MOMENTS

I notice the three men on the platform as I wait for an uptown subway. They are dressed in a combination of elegance and thrift store. One of them has a pretty expensive leather jacket on. Is it warm enough for 30 degrees? Also, his dressy leather shoes are stylish but look outdated by many years. Boots might have served him better. Another has sneakers that almost look clownish. They are simply too big. The men are goodlooking, but worn, and I guess between 40 and 55. Of course, I ease drop as we wait. What else do I have to do? I am a bit tired of reading about the universe and our souls connecting. That is the message, I think, from the Deepak Chopra book in my bag. Maybe it is more about us all being atoms in motion, although we look like solid matter. Or about how each soul matters in the evolution of the universe. Or is it both? And also that we have the capacity to merge into... what was it? Others? The future? Song?

Enough of that deep stuff. The subway train arrives, and we all get on. That includes the three men. I forget about them and drag out the book again. Maybe I can "fathom" another page.

Suddenly, I became aware of singing. Is this the universe in Song? No, it is the three men, who have suddenly become a barbershop quartet! They are good. I am amazed and pleased. So, that is their deal. They get on and off subway cars, singing and collecting change! Oh, oh, the guy with the dressy shoes is coming up to me. I fumble in my bag and find some change. He is pleased as I put it into his hat.

He sings to me, "Give me a kiss, and we can start anew."

I don't recognize the song, but I love the words. I blush a girlish blush even though I am far from girlhood. He nods to me courteously and moves on. The moment passes. But I am still *in* the moment.

Inside, I am smiling and feel warm and cozy and connected to these men, to the strangers in the subway car, and to myself! The smile on my lips and inside me persists. It is lovely. Yes, the universe is suddenly in Song, and I am the Star! What a lovely sensation.

Chapter Twenty-Three

FINDING BLISS

"Bliss is everywhere. You just have to unwrap it." *

This is a wonderful comment, and I would agree. There is potential bliss in so many moments of our lives, if only we know how to get there, instead of "here." Here is being somewhere that is less than blissful. One way to get "there" is to use our memories to retrieve old blissful moments that can be enjoyed and used to create new moments. I talk about this extensively in *The Enchanted Self: A Positive Therapy.* Sometimes these moments are our own. Sometimes they belong to someone else, and we borrow them.

Yesterday, I was talking to my mom's best friend from childhood. My mom, Bernice Becker, is the author of *Feel Good Stories.* This book is full of great memories, but not the one that Betty shared. She told me about how they would spend the summers as youngsters. There was no money for camp in either family, but the two girls had a great time roller skating and going back and forth to the public library. They lived in Brookline,

Massachusetts, on tree-lined streets filled with small apartment buildings and three-family homes. Most apartments had small porches, either in the front facing the street or in the back facing an alleyway or yard. It wasn't heaven, but it was pleasant. The weather was hot, but not as unbearable as weather can be today. They had freedom, exercise, and the next good book to read. Yes, bliss was everywhere those summers. And it was sweet.

How I wish we could all unwrap our bliss every day! And I wish so much that might have been true for my mom, who has since passed. Those days of roller skating and the pleasure of a good novel are so far behind.

*By the way, I heard that saying on TV this morning. It goes with an ad for a new HERSHEY'S chocolate! I guess a good piece of chocolate is another way back to bliss! I could recreate a blissful moment right now by eating a chocolate. I remember how wonderful chocolate tasted when I was a girl, hungry in Girl Scouts camp, and we made Smore's. Should I? Shouldn't I? Mmm. This is a big decision.

Chapter Twenty-Four

SAVORING LIFE

My husband, Russell, and I attended the American Psychological meetings in Boston, Massachusetts. I had gone to graduate school in Boston, so for me, it was my old haunting ground. Also, my mother's family lived there, and I went back and forth to Boston from earliest childhood.

So, of course, every time I'm in Boston, I wander and savor the delights of memory. Yes, I teach about the delights of positive memories in THE ENCHANTED SELF, and yes, I actually do it myself. Milk Street, way downtown Boston, is where my Uncle Cy had his insurance office. Quincy Market is where my boyfriend, who then dropped me, took me for a delicious meal. To my horror, my one and only cap fell out as I ate. A trip to an emergency ward to have the cap put back on finished that evening off. The North End brings back memories of taking a television course at Boston University and walking around with one of the other students as we figured out our television show that we would create. The list goes on and on.

But one of my most important memories is of Filene's Basement. Filene's Department Store was one of my favorite places. I couldn't afford most of the stuff upstairs, but the basement was another matter. All was possible down in the two sub-basements. Incredible sales were just waiting to be had. I would enter a wooden floor paradise of tables overflowing with $2.95 sweaters and raincoats. And if I had more money to spend, I could find a coat for $12.95 and look great in it. Need a wallet? They were there. Ties for my husband? Couldn't beat the quality and the price.

And the wonderful atmosphere; it was a throwback to the 1800s, with the original wood floors and old plain walls. A fire hazard? Maybe, but who cared?

The basement meant so much to me. It was a kind of safe cave of personal adventuring. It was a way to feel excited and pleased at the same time. And when I was done shopping, I could go to Bailey's a few blocks away and have a coffee sundae with hot fudge sauce. Oh, life was sweet.

Last week, my husband and I wandered for hours. Suddenly, we came upon the place where Filene's should have been. Can you imagine my horror to see that it was no more? There was excavating going on all around, and the basement obviously was closed to the public and not functioning. I felt horrible. This was not possible. How could the place where I dreamed and indulged myself just cease to exist? I needed it! It was part of my world!

My husband was indifferent. This was definitely a female response going on.

A few days later, I discovered that Filene's Basement is now a shiny building on a very expensive street near Copley Square. And it is not a basement! I didn't even bother to go in …

Chapter Twenty-Five

HAVING BEST FRIENDS

I remember some special times I had with a best friend, Nancy, when I was growing up. Oh, they were wonderful adventures that we had together — just Nancy and me. And when it came to an end, I had a letdown that could only be compensated for in one way — a long bike ride, a coffee ice cream cone with jimmies on top, and the beginning allure of the next Nancy Drew book. I guess you realize that Nancy Drew was my best friend. Wasn't I lucky?

I think that Nancy Drew was an important icon figure to me, as a positive psychologist, because in the language of Positive Psychology, she gave me hope. She validated that I was smart. She reinforced my resilience. After all, I figured out at least some mysteries before she did. She gave me such a sense of competency. If she could do it, so could I. I just hadn't had the right opportunity yet, so I accompanied her.

She reinforced my strengths and interests. After all, I could figure people out. I could travel, if only my parents would let me. I could act very grown-up and be a leader. Like be on the Student Council. Yes, everything about her was affirming to me. Even her boyfriend gave me hope that someday I would have a boyfriend just as nice and kind and loving, In fact, Nancy Drew was probably the best therapy I had in my life from the ages of 9–11. And she didn't even know she was a Positive Psychologist!

I guess that is why she is so important to the girl in the fiction book, *The Truth: I'm Ten, I'm Smart and I Know Everything.* My character has many of the same feelings about Nancy that I did. She is a bit more competitive with Nancy than I was. But that is ok. Everyone is different. And it is because of Nancy that she has the strength to solve an important mystery that is essential for her growing up happily. But I can't tell. That would give a big secret given away that I want you to read. After all, every author wants her book to be read. So, of course, I can't tell all. I'll just give you one more clue: the mystery involves a locket. Happy reading.

Chapter Twenty-Six

FINDING THE ENCHANTRESS WITHIN PART 1

When I was little, I was very busy — as I imagine most little girls are. At six years of age, I had my toys, my fire station with a real bell, my fire trucks and other cars, my paper dolls, my coloring books, a large box of assorted Crayola crayons, my picture books, and stuffed animals. One of my most important possessions was a "working" toy. A ceramic pig that served as my personal banker. This pig controlled my destiny, to some extent, because when there was enough change inside him, I got to go downtown Bridgeport with my mother and … I picked out a new toy! Now, I was going on seven and saving every penny toward a Toni doll. Did you know you could perm her hair? I couldn't wait!

And then, as if in a flash, I was no longer going on seven but turning 10. A different house, a different town, but still so many interests and passions! I had my hand-held sewing machine and spent hours creating outfits for my dolls. The Toni doll was still around, but unimportant; small Vogue dolls were my passion. I figured out a way to make my own paper patterns for their clothing. I liked my patterns because they involved less sewing than the store-bought doll patterns. That was good for me, since I was interested in adding details such as lace trim more than doing a lot of sewing. The exception to my rule was the bridal gown for my large Vogue doll. I went all out and sewed feverishly, dreaming of a day when ...

I was incredibly busy. I had to practice my violin. I had to read my latest Little Lulu comic. I was in the middle of the Nancy Drew Mystery book that I had convinced my mom to buy me. Oh, I had to work on my next Girl Scout badge by next Thursday. Yes, so much to do and so little time. I'm always at least three days behind in my diary, but I must keep recording my life!

Wash up fast! *I Love Lucy* is on. Everything stops for *I Love Lucy*!

Can you feel the energy — the passion and determination of the child? It might surprise you to realize that the child within each of us, with her energy, her passions, and her potential for greatness is still alive. It may take a trip back in time to find what really sparked us. It may take some creative re-inventing to figure out how we can use the wonderment of our younger self in a form that will work now. But we can get there as our very best friend, that is you, is always waiting to hold our hand and join us in the joyous parts of our energies.

Chapter Twenty-Seven

FINDING THE ENCHANTRESS WITHIN PART 2

I was talking to Nancy Fredericks. She is a corporate consultant and the co-author of a wonderful, empowering book for women, entitled *Dancing on the Glass Ceiling*. As we shared our passion to encourage women to find their strengths and potential (what I call The Song of Your Soul), she shared with me how often she finds that the secret to this personal essence resides in our past.

She remembered herself as a child making potholders. She loved making them, but after a while she had a lot of potholders. She gave some away and still made them. Then she began to think that there had to be a reason for all these potholders! She started selling them to neighbors. They sold! She made more. She got the idea of enrolling her girlfriends in making potholders. It worked. Suddenly she had a big, booming business.

Here she was, a third grader with "the first potholder mass-production line in her neighborhood." She began to make a profit.

In her book, Nancy goes on to say that through recalling this aspect of her childhood, she came in contact with a clue about her Heart's Purpose: "a love of business and a talent for managing people and achieving results."

Nancy's child is so clear. A business entrepreneur in the making! I will have to play with my child and tease out some of the energy that still asks to be cherished in this part of my life. That's OK. I'm not in a rush, and part of recovering our earlier passions — to now live a life that Nancy labels, "Fully Passionate, Fully Alive" — involves time and nurturing.

Why don't you "play" with your child for a while? Pick an age or a couple of ages and get to know that priceless human being again. I suggest that you keep a list of all the talents, strengths, and potential you find as you revisit your younger selves.

Chapter Twenty-Eight

DELIGHTING IN OURSELVES

This is a critical component to general well-being and a sense of happiness on a daily basis. Most of us have sustained loss and experienced pain. Yes, we've been hurt. We've been short-changed by opportunities or other people. Sometimes we've been stepped upon, left, or forgotten.

If we spend our daily life focusing on these disappointments, then we cannot release the positive energies we need to make the most of the present moment and to plan for the future. Grudges, negative thinking, disappointments, and not forgiving all get in the way of what can be done with the present. We need our psychic energies to seize opportunities we can take advantage of. This can't happen if our energies are used up ruminating.

Besides, there is beauty in our own story and most, if not all, disappointments we've experienced have strengthened us.

Often, we have even developed talents in coping with hard times that can reemerge in ways to enhance pleasure and/or help us be of service to the world. For example, the child that was neglected or yelled at has an opportunity to be particularly kind to others. Then as he or she gets older to teach others certain parenting skills, having known firsthand how it feels on the other side.

I suggest you gather the memory gems that make up your own life and begin to sift through them for the stories that are obvious and the stories you may have to dig for. The search will be well worth it. I encourage you to start to share the stories that are unique to your history. My husband and I still enjoy telling the story of when we got food poisoning. It was awful as it was happening but hilarious to retell. And it connects us in a special way to our young married days, graduate school, a vacation that included camping, a ritzy hotel and, best of all, the story connects us to ourselves!

Chapter Twenty-Nine

DARING TO GO BEYOND OURSELVES

Do you know that there is a part of each of us that needs adventure and daring? Boredom is not a healthy state. We all need change and variety. The question is how can we create changes in our lives without disrupting our personal apple cart or taking unnecessary risks? Sometimes, we are hampered by health, sometimes by money, and sometimes we just are too overloaded in our daily patterns of life to build anything new. But still, that innate need for change and variation in our lives will claw at us whether we listen to it or not. I know that I have a desire for stimulation beyond the routines of my life. When I was young, I wanted to meet people from other lands and desperately wanted the adventures of travel. That part of me was slightly satisfied by a pen pal from Wales when I was in high school. But really, I simply still craved travel, and it nagged at me until I went to Europe on my own with a friend at 20. And it still nags at me.

Fortunately, I have discovered as I age that we can often find adventure and new friendships right in front of our noses. Here is an example from my life.

A few years ago, I went to NYC to do my monthly television show, *The Enchanted Self*. I took the subway (or I should say, I tried to take the subway) downtown to Chambers Street to do a bit of shopping beforehand. As I waited on the platform, I saw one of those truly unique characters that could only be either a true eccentric living in NYC or a character actor. Which was he in his frock coat and derby hat? I was so busy imagining! Suddenly, we were on the same train together. He asked how to get to Chambers Street, and I told him. Then I suggested he cross the platform at 14th Street to hop the express, which I was about to do. He did, and that was the beginning of an adventure. First, the subway car started, and we suddenly realized it was going uptown, not downtown. Secondly, he told me that he had to go downtown to Chambers Street to stop in at the new home of *The New York Sun* magazine. He had been hired by them to promote the new paper. Ah! He was a character actor. I was so excited.

I asked him whom he was portraying. He told me that he does Teddy Roosevelt all over the country. His name is James Foote. Well, the next thirty minutes were as if we existed in a dream. He kept going in and out of character. He gave me

Teddy's opinions on the world as it is today — by the way, there was plenty of turmoil 100 years ago! He also explained that Teddy called it the White House. Prior to that, it had been the Executive Mansion! He told me the sad story of how Teddy lost his first wife and mother within a couple of days and how he went into the wilderness for a couple of years to restore his sense of well-being and optimism.

Interesting to me, optimism was one of Teddy's major personality traits. By the way, we were back going downtown again on another train, and I was still listening to Teddy Roosevelt speaking to me! It may have been the hot subway, but it was music to my ears to hear, "Do what you can with, what you've got, and where you are." We certainly had to, as once again we were on the wrong train, and it actually started back uptown at 14th Street. On the third try, we finally emerged at Chambers Street. Mr. Foote reminded me (I never knew this) that the subways were first put in because there had been a snowstorm in NYC that paralyzed the city for weeks. Mr. Roosevelt was significant in getting the subways built. How ironic we were going back and forth on the line affected by 9/11 and as infrequent travelers that neither of us realized most of the trains only went to 14th Street and then started back up. But then, if we had realized this, I wouldn't have had such a great adventure!

I emerged from the underground a changed woman. Imagine Teddy Roosevelt and myself in conversation? (PS: Do you know why Teddy Bears are called Teddy Bears? I do now.)

BUILDING SELF-ESTEEM, PART 1

I was delighted to find out that the passionate woman behind the memoir, *Silver Pages on the Lawn*, is well into her 90s! Somehow that reassures me about my own aging. I was also delighted to find out that a mystery book I just read and loved, *The First Rule of Ten*, is written by a therapist like me.

I am delighted to share my story as an author with you. It began way back when my mother told her dreams every morning and my dad spoke eloquently every day about all items — large and small. It began when I bought the *Girl Scout Diary* with the small lock and key in Reed's department store for myself when I was nine. And it probably began even further back when my mother told me fantastic stories about herself and Melvin, the kid who lived next door that teased her with exaggerated truths. But I'm going to leap ahead to my grown-up days of writing as a professional psychologist. What follows now is part of a paper

I gave at the Norwalk Community College Writer's Conference several years ago:

The famous novelist, Proust stated, "The real voyage for discovery is not in seeking new landscapes but having new eyes." In the 1990s, as a psychologist, I sought new landscapes and was blessed instead with new eyes to see past the disease model to the world of human potential that was right in front of me all the time. I had been researching, via case study methods, women outside my practice to see how women handle childhood messages carried inside them, such as, "You're dumb but beautiful," or "Make sure you get married before your beauty fades." These are discouraging, judgmental messages even if they are not spoken yet are still "heard" clear as a bell. All the women I interviewed concurred with the above premise, giving me many personal examples. However, they had more to teach me. They showed me their strengths, capacities to grow and change and, what most amazed me, their capacities for happiness. These capacities were far beyond what the clinician usually discovers when she is looking through a lens that is primarily sensitive to pathology.

With my *new eyes*, I became certain that women, and I am sure most men, have greater capacities to restore themselves and enjoy themselves than previously documented. I also realized we are not given enough signals in our society to help us feel positive about ourselves or to recognize what makes us happy. We are not taught how to hold on to positive feelings or how to bring them back again and again.

My work appeared to be cut out for me. With my new awareness of what was right about my clients, rather than what was wrong, I was excitedly looking anew at the treatment room. I began to examine how we interact with our clients, how we set the stage for change, how we interview for information, how we teach our clients to view their past behaviors, how we listen, and how we encourage a sense of well-being. I developed techniques for all the above that could be used as a positive overlay for psychologists, regardless of their formal training and orientation. For example, when interviewing a new client, one can easily build in questions that encourage the client to talk about their earlier talents, strengths, lost potential, and resilience. All of these treatment changes in questioning, listening, and processing with the client took shape as *The Enchanted Self: A Positive Therapy.*

Soon, I realized I had a case book in the making. *The Enchanted Self: A Positive Therapy* was published in 1997. The book, utilizing case studies, personal insights from my own life, reader exercises and even poetry, allows the reader to explore positive aspects of herself. If she is a therapist, she also learns how to make long overdue corrections in the treatment room.

Many readers, therapists, and lay people thanked me for the positive paradigm shift I had so clearly outlined in the book. One psychiatrist from Sweden wrote to me that she had waited for years for someone to finally have the courage to make this long overdue correction in therapeutic model.

Chapter Thirty-One

BUILDING SELF-ESTEEM, PART 2

How in the world, as a psychologist and a writer, did I end up writing fiction designed for girls, tweens, teens, moms and grandmas? And how does it dove-tail with *The Enchanted Self: A Positive Therapy*?

Let's look at a poem in *The Enchanted Self: A Positive Therapy* found on page 169: "Come my friend, my nurturer, my shadow, my knowledge of how whole I can be."

Who is that friend? Many years of practicing as a psychologist have convinced me that the nurturer, the shadow, is our earlier selves. Often, it is that self which existed inside us between the ages of 8 and 12. We know that for many girls, 8–12 is a period of soaring, when girls feel competent and so sure of themselves.

If you know girls that age, you know how talented they are. They can and do everything. They also often have special private times, keeping diaries or sharing intimate thoughts with best girlfriends. However, the teenage years do not always encourage or keep girls thriving emotionally and intellectually. The social and hormonal pressures of growing up block the earlier talents and potential. Adolescent years can be very hard on girls, and many a woman finds herself no longer in touch with her earlier talents, strengths, potential, or what makes her happy.

I began to realize that my next psychological assignment was to bring the girl inside ourselves back to life.

I began to develop a companionship with the ten- to eleven-year-old inside myself. I began to realize that as an adult woman that I was disappointing her. I was not as confident or daring as I had promised myself that I would be. Some of my poor decisions had restricted and limited the scope of my potential and opportunities. The girl I had once been knew that the world could be her oyster. She wasn't much afraid of anything and had a lot of inner wisdom. She was resilient and determined. She had faith in me — the adult she would become someday.

Suddenly, getting to know myself as a child again was serious psychological business. It is somewhat painful to realize that one has short-changed herself. Yet, better to realize it now!

Then I began to think, how could I write books that will just spark everyone? If you are a woman, it will make you want to dance with your inner eleven-year-old and make her energies a part of yourself again. If you are a mom, you will see your child in a much more profound light. You will want to help her hold on to her wisdom, wit, sense of competency, and self-esteem. If you are a kid or a tween, you will feel understood and connected to this fictional girl. After all, she is like you. She thinks about many of the things you think about, and she makes promises about what she will be like when she grows up, just like you do.

So, the character came alive. I felt a fictional diary was the way to go. The girl, as many fictional characters do, helped me write the book. She shared her frustrations and her competencies, and she even managed to figure out how she could hold on to the best of herself as she grew up. How she solved the mystery is so endearing, but I can't give it away because I want you to read the book.

She has a crush. Haven't most of us had crushes? I have clients and women in those in workshops as young as five years old having crushes. The girl says, "I am in love... I thought I would fall in love when I was much older, maybe 15 or 16." She explains how she felt when Paul walked into the classroom, "My heart felt like it turned over in my body, my pulse started to race, and I couldn't concentrate. I felt excited, like I had a big secret...."

She also has secrets. She wants to know more about growing up. She wants to ask her mother questions like, "When will I need a bra?" But she can't. "Whenever I try, she looks away and starts to fidget with her fingers. I never get the answers to my questions. Doesn't she know how confused I am?" How is she supposed to be ready to get older if her mother can't tell her everything she needs to know? "Angelina is so lucky because she talks to her mother, Mrs. Allen."

She asks, "Why do grown-ups fight over stupid things? I don't get it. Before you know it, everyone's mood is bad, and the day is ruined...."

Yes, the girl sees so much and knows so much. And didn't we all at 10 or 11? And wouldn't it be great to hold on to the energy and confidence that can go with that stage of life? So that we all can live lives of integrity where we keep similar promises to what the girl makes: "I'll travel a lot. I won't look away when my kids ask me tough questions. I'll answer truthfully. I won't swear. I won't get into silly fights with my husband. I'll have fun with my kids and laugh a lot. I'll remember ME! And that's the truth."

So, you see, I've come full circle with all my books as a positive psychologist. I'm right back to the essence of the person. It turns out that my books for girls are another way of teaching The Enchanted Self. *The Truth: Diary of a Gutsy Tween*, *Secrets: Diary of a Gutsy Teen*, and *Conflict and a Bit of Magic* are all another way of teaching The Enchanted Self. When we come home to the "truth" for ourselves, then we are an Enchanted Self, no matter what our ages are. We are happy; we have purpose. Our lives have meaning. We don't disappoint ourselves. Whether you prefer the casebook or the fictional diaries, it doesn't matter. Just come home to yourself!

Chapter Thirty-Two

FINDING HOLIDAY MAGIC

Holiday blues affect all of us. But, in my opinion, there is no better recipe for offsetting the Holiday blues than being the best you can be.

Below are some tips for improving one's attitude in the coming year:

1. Send a late present to someone you didn't include on your list or give to a charity you pushed aside.

2. Make three New Year's resolutions for yourself. Make one easy, one a little harder, and one a stretch. Fold the paper and keep it in your wallet or pocketbook. Review once a month. Modify if necessary.

3. Make sure you smile every day to at least one person.

4. Compliment at least one person a day and make it real. For example, you may not want to wear that purple scarf on Jane, but you can honestly say it looks good on her.

5. Pay a good deed forward at least once a month, such as paying ahead in line for the person's cup of coffee that is behind you in line.

6. Remember yourself with small treats and time to replenish. You and the world will benefit from you taking care of yourself.

7. Talk to the people in your life, including your kids, without your cell phone in hand.

8. Don't drive and text. Staying alive is essential for all the above.

Chapter Thirty-Three

SELFIES AND SELF-ESTEEM

A news story on the *ABC News* website, entitled "Meet the Dad Who Recorded His Daughter's Epic Selfie Spree," related the story of thirteen-year-old Skylar Beckham who, according to the information, takes about 50 selfies a day. Her father filmed her during one such session and placed the recording on YouTube, where it garnered over one million views.

From my vantage point, as a positive psychologist specializing in girls, tweens and teens, I see Skylar's fascination with herself as very healthy. Her pictures that she sends to her friends are artistic, dramatic, and full of life. They allow her to express, on many levels, personal feelings and facial mannerisms than we typically don't allow in our society. However, the pictures her father took when she was preparing a selfie don't do her a favor. They reveal a private moment that should have stayed private. Selfies should remain the privileged decision of the girl taking them, not the unexpected decision of someone else.

Psychologically, selfies are good for personal development at any age, since they allow us to express, by our choice, extra dimensions of ourselves. Let's keep it that way. These are portraits of ourselves that technology now offers us. Like all technology, we must treat it with respect. In doing so, our kids, and even our grandmas, can "show off" and keep a record of their lives while feeling good about themselves in ways that work for them and certainly don't hurt anyone.

Chapter Thirty-Four

THE POWER OF SELFIES

Everywhere we look today we see "selfies." The most famous selfie ever taken, a celebrity explosion taken by Ellen DeGeneres at the Oscars, made worldwide headlines. Others did not fare so well. While many believe the selfie comes only under the heading of innocent fun, I believe it can serve to help build esteem and to help record our lives. Used inappropriately, however, it can have undesired consequences. What is the difference?

A selfie of yourself engaging in wildly inappropriate behavior is what we in psychology call sliding down the developmental ladder. It can be fun and feel good to do silly things when we are in our private worlds. Regressing is okay and can be even healthy. But taking a selfie when you are in your private space and then putting it on the internet or social media can be dangerous. Why? Because it shows you in a regressed state, and it is out there forever. When you go for a job, what pops up first?

On the other hand, using the selfie concept to share pictures with loved ones or friends of your traveling, celebrating, or anything that is age-appropriate can be good for your and others mental health. Metaphorically, you are now able to hold hands across the miles. For example, the moment you hold your newly adopted new puppy in your arms as he lovingly licks your face, can be engaging and feel good to all concerned. You won't lose a job because you adopted a pet! Lastly, privately using selfies to record a diary, a record of your life that brings you satisfaction, as I have mentioned in a recent article on YourTango, is very healthy. Never before have we had such a quick way to visually capture meaningful moments and memories that enhance our own mental health.

Chapter Thirty-Five

RETRIEVING POSITIVE MEMORIES

I believe that retrieving positive memories is important to our health and well-being. This is one of the dominant themes of my professional teaching. I have come to believe that without a sense that life is pleasant and at times pleasurable, joyful, even rapturous and ecstatic, we are vulnerable to depression, chronic anxiety, and seeing ourselves in a poor light.

My clients and I have found positive information in our own life stories and perk up no matter what the circumstances. For me, perhaps this was never more strongly pointed out than writing *Recipes for Enchantment: The Secret Ingredient is YOU!* Often, when I was writing the book, I remembered and felt the positive lessons that my dad had taught me. I felt his love for me coming through. For example, when I remember his story about how he had not picked up a returnable glass bottle when he was a boy, I am flooded with good feelings about my dad.

My dad really tried to help people to make good decisions. For example, in his story, "That Ain't Worth Nothin,'" he loses a bottle in the gutter because a friend convinces him it is not worth anything. However, the friend then picks it up and turns it in for a "shiny" penny! He loved to tell his lost bottle story because it pointed out occasions that we all face. So often, people try to convince us that something is not good for us. Why? Perhaps because they want it instead, or they really believe it isn't good for us, or for some reason they are blocking us. That's where our personal judgment skill comes into play. Many times, during my life, people have tried to convince me to drop something. For certain there have been people trying to convince me to drop THE ENCHANTED SELF project, as it has been an expensive passion.

Can you imagine? If I had dropped the project, I wouldn't have continued to think about how to help women stay in touch with the best of themselves. And if I had stopped thinking so much about how to help women recapture their zest for living, I wouldn't have started to think more about girls and how important it is for girls to hold on to the best of themselves. And if I hadn't focused a lot on how I could get out the message to girls about growing up emotionally strong, I never would have written and published *The Truth: I'm Ten, I'm Smart and I Know Everything*. And if I had never written that book, I wouldn't have gotten the idea for the second book in The Truth Series: *SECRETS, (You tell me yours, maybe I'll tell you mine)*. And if none of the above had happened… well, it wouldn't be the same for me or lots of people that my books and theories have touched.

Chapter Thirty-Six

FLYING HORSES

The Baal Shem Tov was a rabbi who lived in the 18th century. He had extraordinary powers to uplift the down-trodden Jewish populations of Eastern Europe. As most of the Jews in Europe at that time, The Baal Shem Tov lived in a small Jewish village. However, he had so much to teach, and he was so eager to help Jews everywhere (it was reported he not only helped but miracles often happened after a meeting with him) that he could not confine himself to his village.

After Shabbos each week, he would hitch his horses to his wagon and would set out for somewhere else to help or inspire other Jews. It was said that it was an absolute miracle that he was able to get around all around Russia, which was a giant country, and yet get back to his village in a timely fashion.

It was purported that the way that he did this was as follows: After he left his village and no one was watching, he would encourage his horses, and they would begin to fly. Because they were flying, they were able to cover incredible distances. Once he reached a particular town and was able to help someone or give someone critical advice or a special blessing that might even lead to a miracle happening, he would then set out for his town.

Again, once no one was looking, he would nudge the horses lightly, and they would begin to fly. And he did this repeatedly, week after week. Meanwhile, it was said that the horses would talk to each other while they were flying. One horse would say to the other, "Do you realize that we are flying?" The other horse would answer and say, "Yes, we are flying. This is amazing!" Then the first horse would say, "We must be extremely special. We must be like the angels because we are able to fly." And the other horse said, "You know, you're right! We must be just as good as angels since we can fly." And they would banter back and forth with conversation as they flew through the skies.

But it was also said that once they got back to earth and a bag of oats was put on each horse's nose, they ate just like horses. There was nothing going on that was elevating or different from any horse eating. They were not like angels. They were simply two horses eating their oats.

What is the message that this story is trying to teach us?

The message is that the horses, even though they could fly, were still just animals. For us, as human beings, we may or may not feel that we are flying, but we always have the opportunity to raise ourselves up toward the heavens. We can elevate ourselves in the ways that we conduct ourselves, so that whether we are eating a meal, befriending someone, going to work, talking to a neighbor, whatever it is no matter how small and no matter how routine, we have the opportunity to elevate our acts and demonstrate our sense of self-esteem. Our acts can be caring, helpful, kind, sensitive, refined, timely, thoughtful. And the list goes on. So, as humans, we are always approaching the angels if we will only bother to elevate ourselves.

Elevation homework for you: How can you begin to elevate yourself and build self-esteem this week in three small ways? One might be as simple as smiling and asking a neighbor how he is, or you might let someone go in front of you in line at the supermarket, or you might listen to what someone is saying while not multi-tasking literally or in your mind. Good luck with flying this week!

Chapter Thirty-Seven

WOULD YOU INVITE ANTS TO YOUR PICNIC?

Would you? I'm sure you would prefer not to! So, my question to you is why would you invite people that are unpleasant and/or not in your best interest into your life? Sometimes, it happens because someone intimidates us. Sometimes we think someone is a wonderful addition to our lives, and then as time goes by, we realize otherwise! Certainly, the experience of an unwelcome guest at our "picnic" is a universal happening. I am talking about our lives. Our "picnics" are a metaphor for each of our lives. And what a delight our lives should be! Just like a wonderful picnic, each day should be a great daily event where the food is wonderful, the weather is sunny, and people who respect and care about us are our guests. Laughter and wisdom should prevail, along with kindness, interest in others, and positive energy. Feelings of delight should have guest passes! So, how do we get rid of those nasty ants walking on our beautiful red and white checkered picnic cloth? Let's talk about two different types of invaders. The first are people who are simply not in your best interest. They may appear as friends or even be your relatives, but you know at some profound gut level that they are not invested in your well-being as much as you would expect for whatever the level of connection is. The second type of invader is the person who seems to drain you of your energy. Talking to one of them for five minutes may make you feel exhausted or depleted for the rest of the day. Sometimes, you don't know what hits you, it happens so fast. How do we push back from both types of people? Of course, the answers can be extremely complicated if one of these invaders may be your boss, or a close relative, or a friend of your dearest friend, etc. Often, we cannot just dismiss these people from our lives. But here are a few suggestions:

1. If someone is draining your energies, you can imagine a protective shield around you when you are with them. Perhaps you can think of a plastic shield that surrounds you.

2. Make sure with someone that drains you that you don't spend extra time together if you can avoid it.

3. When people are not in your best interest you may find it helpful to genuinely take a real interest in them. Focusing on them when you chat will not only make them feel good but may actually change their attitude toward you. Some people are

simply not in your best interest because they feel competitive and even envious. So, if they feel you really care about them, in an instant they relax and begin to care about you!

4. For more serious negative invaders of your success in life, you may have to truly distance yourself. This can be as dramatic as not seeing someone anymore or may simply mean learning how to get off the phone quickly when you have to talk to them. Of course, at this level of separation, you may need counseling or psychotherapy to help you protect yourself and distance.

Chapter Thirty-Eight

GOING BEYOND LOSS

Some of you know that my mother passed away. I miss her so much. Sometimes I feel she is still right here with me. One example is when I sat down to write my latest book, a romance-mystery novel for women. I often feel that she is helping me write it. She was a wonderful writer and much more into fiction than I. Most of her life she read two or three books a week. I thought it would be interesting to share with you a story she wrote about her own mom's passing. It is a magical story. You can decide for yourself how you would interpret what she experienced.

Building resilience and self-esteem are very important, and even more so when dealing with major life changes such as the death of a family member.

Stranger Than Fiction* by Bernice Becker

My mother was gone. She would not come back. She could not come back. She had passed on in Noble Hospital in Westfield with me, unbelieving and distraught, at her side. There was a sad, dignified funeral because Uncle Dave, her brother, would not have it any other way. He was a strong, good, and domineering man whom she had respected and adored. She was buried next to my dad and close to her very caring and devoted family.

Here I was, sitting in her favorite outdoor chair near the front stoop of our house, looking up at the clear blue sky and pleading with God to let me see her even for a little while. I needed to tell her how important she had been in my life and how much I missed her. Her passing had been quick and unexpected in spite of health problems.

I believed that if I concentrated enough and prayed fervently, I might see her walking toward me in the driveway, where she often strolled on bright, sunny days. She had lived with us during the last two years of her life, while her heart weakened gradually until it gave out. Harry and I had promised Uncle Dave we would keep her with us instead of in a nursing home. He hated nursing homes with a passion.

Finally, I decided this was not the day she would come home — maybe next time. Reluctantly, I entered my home to prepare dinner and spend time with our ten-year-old daughter, who needed my attention as well as my love. She felt the loss but not to the extent of my understandable grief.

A few months later, I began to dream frequently that I was with my mother. She appeared as herself, except more cheerful than in life and not aware she was deceased. I was afraid to say, "Mother, do you know you are dead?" That's a delicate subject even in a dream for me. However, the time finally came when I dared to use those words.

She argued with me and scolded me for making such a foolish remark to a person who was alive.

I dropped the subject.

In my dreams, we walked and talked, shopped, and spent time in the restaurants I had often taken her to for her favorite dessert, warm apple pie and ice cream.

Then something began to happen that I could not fathom. I was in a deep sleep in the double bed I shared with my husband. It seemed every time I started to bring myself out of that state, my mom was lying next to me. Harry was not there. I could see her blue dotted Swiss nightgown. I felt the soft material next to me. I touched her wavy silver hair and listened to how softly she breathed. She smiled at me. Logically, I knew she wasn't there. When I finally forced myself fully awake, Harry was beside me and everything was back to normal.

This unusual experience was repeated countless times, not for days, weeks, or months but over a period of at least five years. I mentioned this only to my husband and a close friend. The response was "You're dreaming. You are imagining. Don't dwell on it. Let her go."

I implored her, "You must leave. You have to join Papa and your family who love you and are expecting you." She said, "I can't leave until my brother Dave is there too."

About six months after those words, Uncle Dave died of a complication following surgery. The next time I was with my mother I stated emphatically, "Your time has come to leave. Your dear brother died, and he is waiting for you. He was always so good to you; you must not disappoint him."

She inquired, "Are you positive he is dead?"

"I would not lie about anything like that. Believe me."

"All right, I will go. I don't want Dave to be angry with me."

We were in a large, unfamiliar bedroom where sheer white curtains were blowing gently next to an open window. She was sitting in a chair wrapped in a lightweight blanket. She asked me to carry her over to the window. She was almost weightless in my arms. I felt as though I were the mother and she the child. She told me "I love you, but now I must go away." She floated out of my arms. It was a balmy night, and the midnight sky was lit with brilliant stars. She kept looking back and waving.

I waved back and called out, "I love you; be happy."

She called out; "I love you, too, dear." She slowly disappeared from my view. I was happy for her.

That morning when I woke up, I felt free, as though a weight had been lifted. Harry was beside me. Those dreams stopped, never to return. Now, I am able to have the normal dreams one expects.

More than twenty years since, I still wonder what it all meant. Was my mother's spirit wandering between heaven and earth? Was she unwilling to leave Uncle Dave and me, or did my subconscious mind refuse to let her go? It is a mystery that may never be solved. Perhaps in many years, I will have my answer, but I'm not in any hurry to find out.

Chapter Thirty-Nine

OWNING OUR PASSIONS

As women, we must honor our true passions. If we don't, we are unhappy, even depressed. I've talked about this concept for years. In *The Enchanted Self: A Positive Therapy*, I discuss many reasons why we need to be true to ourselves. I will also explain why we cannot wait for anyone else to do this job for us. We MUST take care of ourselves. As it has been said, your best friend and your most devoted partner came into your life on the day you were born. And that person was not your mom. It was you.

I'm always looking for women who are living out their dreams. They are wonderful, magical women who fill us with hope and encouragement. They feel magical because they have taken the best of themselves from various stages of their lives and integrated these special parts of themselves into a new whole that is even better. For example, the woman I met in Wales who took her love of fairy tales as a child and her business sense as a woman and opened a store selling princess outfits and magic wands to little girls, took the best of herself from childhood and adulthood.

Are you one of those special women who has taken something special about yourself from the past and brought it to life in a new way now, as an adult? I bet you have. Write back and let me know and give us all the details!

Chapter Forty

MEETING OUR NEEDS

The Enchanted Self's Third Gateway to Happiness is all about learning to meet our needs, and how to negotiate for ourselves. Often, kids certainly know what their needs are better than adults, because everything is less disguised, fresher and closer to the surface. But they very often don't know how to negotiate for themselves or how to find ways to get their needs met, particularly if they live in difficult families. So, we have to help them again.

Advice for young women in this category, how they might be able to sort of go around difficult circumstances and manage:

Get mentors outside the household. A neighbor who's really a good person, who maybe you can go over and the two of you can cook together in her kitchen now and then. It can be a teacher that takes an interest in you. Perhaps she introduces you to fine literature, or she finds a young piano teacher so you can take lessons at a price your parents can afford. I don't mean a formal mentor like we think of in coaching where you pay someone by the hour. I simply mean someone who sees you in a positive light and enriches your life in positive ways.

I'm talking about people who can take you beyond your family circumstances.

Chapter Forty-One

POSITIVE PSYCHOLOGY FOR WOMEN ONLY

My search for what I call THE ENCHANTED SELF began many years ago when, after many years in private practice, an urge was building within me to learn more about how the messages girls receive in childhood about who they should become interface later with their sense of self in adulthood. I wanted a firsthand sense of how ordinary women handle a profound array of messages given to them in childhood. I anticipated somewhat despairing findings, having worked for many years with women in my private practice who reported negative and destructive messages from family members, lovers, husbands — messages that were in dissonance with a woman's often fragile sense of self.

For example, I'll never forget the strength of emotion behind the voice of my client as she talked about her husband who would squelch every good idea, which she brought up by saying, "And that and five cents will get you a cup of coffee."

To do this project I developed a structure interview, which I administered to 18 non-client women, ranging in age from 35 to 75. I took extensive notes during each interview, as well as audio taped each survey participant. All of them were white, middle to upper middle class, Christian or Jewish. Several had psychotherapy. Most had not.

This was case study data done by myself at my own expense to give me a broader sense of women's development. I did not attempt to have a statistically random group of women but, rather, worked in a reality situation where friends recommended other friends who might participate in the structured interview.

My interview questions were geared toward gaining insight into how the messages girls received in childhood about the role they were to play in society influenced their adult development. I was also interested in if a woman was or had been married, whether she had experienced criticism in the marriage relationship, and how this experience influenced the way she felt about herself. I had initially included a question geared toward asking the women when they felt most whole in adulthood. However, as I interviewed the women and became increasingly aware of the enhanced reports they gave me of good times and feelings, new questions emerged. My structured interview evolved to include other questions such as when the women felt most whole, most centered, in girlhood. The major questions were:

1. What messages did you absorb in girlhood about the role you were to play in society as a grown up woman some day?

2. What were some unspoken, perhaps secret, but understood messages you absorbed in girlhood about women? How did these messages affect your girlhood?

3. Talk about your family life as you remember it from girlhood. How did the family operate emotionally? What were some family rules, messages, and what part did each member play?

4. What were times in your girlhood when you felt most centered—when you felt a childhood sense of wholeness, well-being? Tell me about some of these memories.

5. Can you reflect on times in your womanhood when you have felt most whole, flowing, integrated, alive — when you know that you are following your own inner sense of well-being?

6. Can you link in any way any of your adult times of enhanced self with earlier moments when you felt whole, centered, in a special flow? ...

It was gratifying and exhilarating to discover that without focused production time and without any public recognition — both essential values in the American concept of "success" — these ordinary women had found so many ways to have an enhanced adult life experience. These ways were often secret, at least in the sense that these women did not typically think of talking about their heightened moments or creating artistic forms around them. These women were too tired, too busy, too preoccupied, and too worried about a multitude of tasks. However, some by conscious decisions, others by what seemed to be unconscious process, had permitted their enhanced selfhoods to emerge whenever it was reasonably possible to do so, without jeopardizing the other tasks they considered essential, such as mothering, providing an income, being a wife, etc.

This unexpected finding surprised me. Yet, I found myself captivated by the theme of personal capacities for well-being and pleasure. In fact, I was more captivated than by the original thrust of my investigation.

As a therapist, I was developing a new hypothesis: many of our clients may have, in spite of the destructiveness of the cultural environment, experienced times of adult enhancement — moments and/or periods of time when there is a return to some sense of self-worth, a feeling of joy, a sense of bliss. This is a special place within oneself that each person can recognize, although it is easily overlooked. I began to call this place "The Enchanted Self." Later, as I used the term in writings, in teaching, and in the treatment room, I was told how appreciative women often were that I had given a name to this special place within ourselves that is so often ignored, dismissed, and/or devalued.

Further definition emerged. The Enchanted Self is a unique reservoir of wellness that resides in each human being. It is specific to that person's memory bank and unique experiences. Once tapped into, we experience a state of well-being that may include positive feelings, thoughts, sensations, both cognitive and in the body. The woman may become aware of a sense of integrity and self-integration. Sometimes we experience this place while alone and other times while in connective experiences. This place permits a profound sense of feeling centered and whole. When we are there, we recognize it. I remain convinced that girlhood messages are profoundly important in terms of adult female development, at times in clearly dysfunctional ways....

Chapter Forty-Two

FINDING MIDLIFE ENCHANTMENT

An enchanted life is created and begins from within us. We reawaken our enchantment through knowing what the heart and authentic soul of our desires is. By the time women hit midlife, many of us have focused so much of our energy on doing for others that we lose touch with what is meaningful, important, special, magnificent, intimate, and magical to us... and most important, WHY it is so.

Getting connected to our enchanted child guides us to the heart and soul of our desires. When we have that piece of knowledge, that spark, we have the enchanted core of our desires. The universal law of attraction then can begin to work and will attract more of that into your life.

STEP 1) What activities did you really enjoy in childhood? Let your mind recall times when you felt enchanted. When you forgot what time it was, when you were creating something, felt involved, juiced, excited. Make a list of as many as you can remember. They can be very simple snippets in time like the example of swinging.

STEP 2) Go there in your imagination and re-experience the enchantment that swinging had for you.

STEP 3) Ask yourself: What feeling did it give me when I was swinging? What about it tickled you? We Pokies want to get to the "feeling place" underneath the activity. That's where the magic is.

* Using the example of swinging, it may have given you a feeling of incredible freedom.

STEP 4) Let's just say it was the feeling of freedom. What does freedom mean to you? What qualities does freedom have for you? Where do you experience this feeling in your body? Breathe into it and ask it for more information. Let your authentic feeling of freedom speak to you and give you more information.

* The feeling of freedom that swinging gave you may have associations of being unrestricted and unobstructed.

STEP 5) What else conjures up that feeling within you? What do you associate with that feeling of freedom? Is there any place in your adult life where you get that feeling? What are you doing? What is giving you that feeling? Where in your adult life do you want and need more of that? What is the next logical step for someone in your position now that you have discovered more about your authentic soul's voice?

Chapter Forty-Three

FINDING YOUR ENCHANTED SELF

What are the tools to get to THE ENCHANTED SELF part of ourselves? What skills do we need in order to find happiness that is unique and sustainable for each person?

I suggest you enter the Seven Gateways of Happiness that go with THE ENCHANTED SELF and find the tools waiting for you at each Gateway. Let's look at the first Gateway:

First Gateway: Honoring what is Right about Ourselves Rather Than What is Wrong

As women, we're all experts in identifying what is wrong with ourselves. We can probably quickly make up a long list, detailing what is wrong in our lives. However, it's a lot harder to get in touch with what is right. We need to know ourselves in positive ways. We need to learn how to honor our talents, strengths, even our coping skills which serve us so well. And most important, we need to treasure and enjoy our potential.

These parts of us, if not honored, identified and talked about both to ourselves and to others, will lose their power. We have to keep igniting them. We need to get to know ourselves in ways that emphasize the heroic, strong parts of ourselves. This means using our memories in very different ways from what we've been accustomed to. It means searching through our history to find our talents, strengths, and even lost potential, even if we have to sort through pounds of dysfunction. It means searching our past for what is right about ourselves, not for what is wrong. Each of us is capable of doing the above. For a starter, take a sheet of paper and list some of your talents, strengths, and potentials from several different times in your life. Look for realistic items, not ones that would get you into the Olympics. For example, let's say you pick the seventh grade to look at. Maybe you were good at making friends, a B student and had the potential to be a good pianist if you had a chance. These are realistic talents, strengths, and potential.

Chapter Forty-Four

DREAMING

In my book, *Recipes for Enchantment: The Secret Ingredient is YOU!*, I talk about so many occasions when people took positive actions and then had the pleasant rewarding experience of positive feelings. These positive feelings varied from person to person yet included the whole spectrum of well-being, including: joyousness, contentment, satisfaction, pleasure and, on occasion, rapture.

In my book, I share a reverie that I had one night. I imagined all of my friends and loved ones and then strangers from around the world coming together in big circles dancing in the moonlight. We danced until dawn. There was a sense of euphoria that built up, leading to me experiencing great joy and even rapture as I indulged in my visualization. I share this one with you because it points out that positive actions can take the form of positive thoughts! Often, we dismiss our inner life. I think it's important to document that our inner life is a very real place where we practice many of the states of well-being that ultimately take shape through expression in the real world.

Although I have not danced through the night in the moonlight with hundreds of thousands of people, the feelings I had in that reverie certainly translated into many of the positive actions that I take in sharing THE ENCHANTED SELF message. As a matter of fact, without my inner life, I doubt there would be the energy to bring these teachings to others.

Yes, obviously in this discussion we are moving toward the spiritual. Ultimately, the positive energies that we have to give the world require mind, body, and spirit. You see, enchantment is all about putting the meat in your soul's soup. It is about the muscle that goes with living a life of joy. Perspiration, daily practice, and daily routines that enhance the possibilities of living a life of enchantment, are all of hard work.

Just remember though, before you get discouraged, it is even harder to live a miserable life. We pay for misery in so many ways. We pay for it by feeling fatigued and feeling that we don't have real purpose. We feel inside that there's a hole in our hearts or that we have missed the boat. We can feel aggravated, tense, and fed up. We can feel that the future will be as miserable as the past. We can feel that we are ordinary rather than extraordinary. We can pay for a negative attitude with more physical and emotional illness so that the perspiration pours off of us in a different way.

I think it's smarter, since life is a struggle and designed so that we work at whatever we're doing, that we practice enchantment and enjoy the perspiration and inspiration that goes with the practice. So, promise yourself to take the JOYRIDE OF YOUR LIFE!

Chapter Forty-Five

RESTORING YOURSELF AGAIN AND AGAIN

How do we take all the moments of life that are often repetitive and ordinary and turn them into captivating personal times? One way is through optimizing our own sense of well-being. This internal state is particularly reactive to our emotional and physical states of health. For instance, I remember occasions when good things were about to happen, but I was so over-tired or anxious that I could not appreciate a special day. I also remember occasions when nothing happened, but because I felt well rested and truly at peace with myself, I enjoyed every moment.

How do we work on restoring ourselves? How do we gather our positive energies to be in our own best interest? Certainly, one of the most critical factors is seeing yourself in a positive light. If I don't truly value myself, I am certainly not going to take good care of myself. I am more responsive to the criticism from a negative spouse or parent than my own inner feelings of self-worth. I may not take good care of myself, and the results can be devastating. Over the years, I have seen so many clients who were not thriving because they had internalized negative comments, criticism, and opinions from others. The end result was that they began to believe in the negative perceptions of themselves and ultimately saw themselves in a poor light.

It is very important to see yourself in a positive light. This means not putting yourself down and not criticizing yourself. It means becoming your own best friend. Often, taking better care of yourself becomes essential. For all of us, it is important to get enough rest, eat well, learn how to sort through the negative remarks that hurt, not get caught up and lost in the feelings those remarks engendered, and to value who we really are and what each of us has to offer the world.

This "R" is extremely difficult and involves a lot of mental and emotional perspiration. We are vulnerable to absorbing criticism and negative remarks about ourselves and actually internalizing them Pokies, making them ours. So, there is much work to be done when we start to sift through feelings that we are less rather than more. We need to think of ourselves as more, not less.

I remember one client who had struggled to think of herself as more, not less. Her husband was often critical of her and was constantly interruptive. For example, when eating out, he would often criticize her and spoil her pleasure by suggesting she had put on some pounds and might not want to order a particular item. Around the house, he would barge into a room and interrupt her telephone conversation or television show. He would then bring up a subject and present her as the culprit.

It was a wonderful day in her life when she was simply able to say when he interrupted her, "I am leaving the house for a few hours. I hope upon my return your mood will be better, and you will be treating me more appropriately." She then took the car keys and went to visit a friend. When she came back, he was pleasant and in a totally different state. Although this was only part of the correction between them, it was a decisive moment in giving her a sense that not only must she think of herself as more, not less, but she also must have the courage to take positive appropriate action.

Rapture is a strong, full word that incorporates a capacity for joy that affects us in our own mind, body, and spirit. It is a feeling of being in harmony in a euphoric or an ecstatic way with others or the universe at large. Obviously, we don't go around in a state of rapture all the time. To experience even states of well-being on a regular basis involves tremendous daily practice. Yet, if we work and perspire mentally, emotionally, and socially we will be rewarded. How? For one thing, the positive actions we take in our lives are pleasing to us and good for us.

Chapter Forty-Six

REMEMBERING THE BEST

In today's world, there are so many wonderful and inspirational books. There are books filled with stories of Divine intervention, miracles happening, special positive moments never to be forgotten, and stories of incredible coincidences. They help make us feel in harmony with the universe. They help us fall asleep and have pleasant dreams. They often bring tears to our eyes, reinforcing an inner sense of wisdom that all is right with the world even when appearances say that is not so.

But there is one thing often missing from these books. It is the mental and emotional perspiration that we need to go through as we struggle to live a life of meaning and joy. The inspiration is there, but it's the perspiration that most of us need to put into our daily lives to create for ourselves lives of enchantment. Because, for most of us, enchantment, i.e., living a life of joy, a life that reflects many states of well-being, again and again is hard work.

Certainly, we yearn for moments when the right thing happens at exactly the right time and the world opens up for us, whether it's a lucky break, meeting the right life partner, or winning the lottery. And we all need at least some of those moments. But life, in reality, is filled with hundreds and thousands and probably millions of minutes that are repetitive, boring, or simply ordinary. They involve getting up, brushing our teeth, driving to work safely, keeping a job, raising children, fighting off a cold, etc. It is all these times that THE ENCHANTED SELF focuses on.

These are the moments that can be "Buy Cialis®" mundane, depressing, and dull or captivating, enlivening, and filled with joy.

What is the difference? The difference is usually perspiration, meaning the mental and emotional perspiration that is involved in what I call the three R's of enchantment. Let's look at the first of the three R's.

The first is REMEMBERING THE BEST AND LETTING GO OF THE REST. This is a critical component to general well-being and a sense of happiness on a daily basis. Most of us have sustained loss and experienced pain. Yes, we've been hurt. We've been shortchanged by opportunities or other people. Sometimes, we've been stepped upon, left, or forgotten.

If we spend our daily life focusing on these disappointments, then we cannot release the positive energies we need to make the most of the present moment and to plan for the future. Grudges, negative thinking, disappointments, and not forgiving all get in the way of what can be done with the present. We need our psychic energies to seize opportunities we can take advantage of. This can't happen if our energies are used up ruminating.

Besides, there is beauty in our own story and most, if not all, disappointments we've experienced have strengthened us. Often, we have even developed talents in coping with hard times that can reemerge in ways to enhance pleasure and/or help us be of service to the world. For example, the child that was neglected or yelled at has an opportunity to be particularly kind to others as he or she gets older, maybe to teach others certain parenting skills, having known firsthand how it feels on the other side.

Chapter Forty-Seven

HONORING OUR TRUE PASSIONS

As women, we have to honor our true passions. If we don't, we are unhappy, even depressed. I've talked about this concept for years. In *The Enchanted Self: A Positive Therapy*, I discuss many reasons why we need to be true to ourselves. I also explain why we cannot wait for anyone else to do this job for us. We MUST take care of ourselves. As it has been said, your best friend and your most devoted partner came into your life on the day you were born. And that person was not your mom. It was you.

I'm always looking for women who are living out their dreams. They are wonderful, magical women who fill us with hope and encouragement. They feel magical because they have taken the best of themselves from various stages of their lives and integrated these special parts of themselves into a new whole that is even better. For example, the woman I met in Wales, who took her love of fairy tales as a child and her business sense as a woman and opened a store selling princess outfits and magic wands to little girls, took the best of herself from childhood and adulthood.

Are you one of those special women who has taken something special about yourself from the past and brought it to life in a new way now, as an adult? I bet you have.

Chapter Forty-Eight

FINDING BLESSINGS

Hi, Ladies. I hope you are having a beautiful day today. Don't we all need to! Do you feel better when someone has blessed you? I sure to. It makes me feel cared about in a special way when I know someone has blessed me. I'd like to know how you feel about blessings? Did you ever have a really special day after someone blessed you? A blessing can be as simple as "Take care." Or it can be much more, such as the blessings I have listed below from my e-mail blessings that I send out once a week. By the way, you can sign up for my blessings by going to the front page of https://www.enchantedself.com .

Enjoy these four blessings, Pokies, and please send me a blessing by giving me the blessing of your response! Write to me here on this blog or at drbarbara@enchantedself.com

"May you be blessed with a disposition that is just as sunny in the rain as in the sun."

"May the wonders of technology always be a boon to your life, and may you have the courage to not let these wonders 'bust' your integrity, time, or need for genuine privacy and intimate connection that cannot be had by turning on an electrical current."

"May you always be pleased with freedom, both inside and outside yourself!"

"May all that befalls you be delicious and filled with delight even if at first you are puzzled or dismayed!"

Chapter Forty-Nine

TAKING EASY STEPS TO ENCHANTMENT

An enchanted life is created and begins from within us. We reawaken our enchantment through knowing what the heart and authentic soul of our desires is. By the time women hit midlife, many of us have focused so much of our energy on doing for others that we lost touch with what is meaningful, important, special, magnificent, intimate, and magical to us.... and most important, WHY it is so.

Getting connected to our enchanted child guides us to the heart and soul of our desires. When we have that piece of knowledge, that spark, we have the enchanted core of our desires. The universal law of attraction then can begin to work and will attract more of that into your life.

STEP 1) What activities did you really enjoy in childhood? Let your mind recall times when you felt enchanted. When you forgot what time it was, when you were creating something, felt involved, juiced, excited. Make a list of as many as you can remember. They can be very simple snippets in time like the example of swinging.

STEP 2) Go there in your imagination and re-experience the enchantment that swinging had for you.

STEP 3) Ask yourself: What feeling did it give me when I was swinging? What about it tickled you? We Pokies want to get to the "feeling place" underneath the activity. That's where the magic is.

* Using the example of swinging, it may have given you a feeling of incredible freedom.

STEP 4) Let's just say it was the feeling of freedom. What does freedom mean to you? What qualities does freedom have for you? Where do you experience this feeling in your body? Breathe into it and ask it for more information. Let your authentic feeling of freedom speak to you and give you more information.

* The feeling of freedom that swinging gave you may have associations of being unrestricted and unobstructed.

STEP 5) What else conjures up that feeling within you? What do you associate with that feeling of freedom? Is there any place in your adult life where you get that feeling? What are you doing? What is giving you that feeling? Where in your adult life do you want and need more of that? What is the next logical step for someone in your position now that you have discovered more about your authentic soul's voice?

* You may be a person who needs to feel in charge of your own time, money, projects, decisions, and energy at work, so you may need to be your own boss. Working by someone else's time clock and directives may make you feel that constricted feeling, and you may not even know where it is coming from. Unfortunately, many of us think there is something wrong with us and try to "deal" with our discomfort.

Chapter Fifty

NANCY DREW AND YOU AND THE TRUTH

If you are at all like many girls and women in the United States, Nancy Drew served as an important figure in your life at one time or another. For me, she was VERY important when I was nine, ten, and even eleven. I would wait with high anticipation if I knew my mother was coming home from shopping and might have a new Nancy Drew book with her. If she did, my next week would surely be close to heaven. I would have a mystery to solve along with Nancy and all the positively luscious feelings of excitement I would be bound to feel as I accompanied her on her newest adventure. Forget her close buddies, they were only silly girls. I was as dedicated as she was to solving mysteries, and I was there for her. Oh, it was a wonderful adventure — whatever it was. And when it came to an end, I had a letdown that could only be compensated in one way — a long bike ride and the beginning allure of the next Nancy Drew book.

I think that Nancy Drew was an important figure to me because, in terms of Positive Psychology, she gave me hope. She validated that I was smart. After all, I figured out at least some mysteries before she did. She gave me a sense of competency. If she could do it, so could I. I just hadn't had the right opportunity yet, so I accompanied her.

She reinforced my strengths and interests. I could figure people out. I could travel, if only my parents would let me. I could act very grown-up and be a leader. After all, I was on the student council. Yes, everything about her was affirming to me. Even her boyfriend gave me hope that someday I would have a boyfriend just as nice and kind and loving. In fact, Nancy Drew was probably the best therapy I had in my life from ages nine to eleven. And she didn't even know she was a Positive Psychologist!

Chapter Fifty-One

SELF ESTEEM THROUGH MEMORY

It has been commonly known in the mental health field that in order to achieve good mental health, a person needs self-esteem. However, what has not been stressed adequately is the importance of our memories. Often, memories are encouraged that help us recall what has not worked in our life, what was dysfunctional, or disappointing. We don't emphasize enough how to use our memories to recall what has given us pleasure and wisdom in the past to see if we can reincorporate an old activity or interest or find a way to transform it into something that will work at whatever stage of life we are at.

As a Positive Psychologist and Originator of a method designed to encourage hope, optimism, happiness, resiliency, purpose, and meaning in life, I always teach people how to retrieve the positive parts of their memories and celebrate the true heroine that each of us is. I find that if we take the time to learn how to read, as a blueprint, the dysfunctional times in our lives, to see what strengths and survival skills stand out, we can celebrate the powerful woman inside, even if the times around the memories were less than ideal.

THE ENCHANTED SELF is a Positive Psychology that encourages positive states of mind, body, and spirit. It is a growth-promoting system of positive understandings and attitudinal changes, insights, and simple lifestyle changes you can make. It is geared to living a life more joyfully and fully. It is a way of seeing the glass half full, and it's a way of seeing yourself as extraordinary rather than ordinary. It's a way of recognizing the heroine within yourself. You see that your own personal memories contain not only your history of the story of your life, but there is a wealth of wisdom with which to reinvent yourself again and again.

You are the only person who has had your unique experiences, human reactions, and thoughts. You are the holder of the key to your own enchantment. It is out of your past that you can find coping skills, ability, talent and lost potential. Only you can determine what you enjoy and what gives you a sense of well-being.

Chapter Fifty-Two

PRACTICING GRATITUDE

Gratitude is a marvelous practice, yet as a positive psychologist I have to share my clinical experiences. It is not an easy practice! When we are down, whether we are grieving, sad, hurt, or maybe, unfortunately, a combination of these difficult feelings, we are not interested in running through a list of what has worked in our lives or even how we have grown. I often suggest to people that during these times we try the mental health gift of positive action.

Whether we force ourselves to say hello to someone and admire their outfit or hairdo, or whether it comes easily to do a favor of someone, just giving out instead of going back inside ourselves will improve our state of mind. It may not work instantly, but it will work. Since New Year's, I've been practicing saying, "Happy New Year" to strangers. They are pleased, although sometimes surprised. Me, I have felt good for many moments when I might not have otherwise! Try it, you'll like it.

Chapter Fifty-Three

FINDING PLEASANT MEMORIES

Each season requires special behaviors and activities to optimize living a purposeful and happy life. We actually have to practice our positive emotions, just as the champion tennis player practices her swing. We have to try to use our mental capacities as fully as possible, our cognitive capacities for thought, and our emotional capacity to practice positive feelings and emotions. Actually, if we allow it, the seasons help us to live a full and meaningful life. The seasons even give us the "recipes for happiness" that we can cook up if we just look around and recognize what each time of year has to offer.

For example, autumn is a season of memory for most of us. Most people have attended the next grade in school growing up, as the first leaves begin to fall. For myself, not only do the turning leaves, the sight of a pumpkin, and the fresh, crisp, clear smell of a cool day conjure up positive memories of childhood, but symbols tied into traditions also inspire me. For many, the major symbols of a fall holiday are not until Halloween pumpkins begin to appear. But for those of us who are Jewish, the traditional symbols of our fall holidays almost always stir up good feelings and memories. In my case, I'm talking about positive memories that were not personally mine, but nevertheless I lived through them by my grandmother telling me of her childhood.

Every year, I would make my grandmother tell me about the Sukkots they had when she was growing up in Chelsea, Massachusetts. The Sukkah is a hut or a room where the roof can be partly opened so that you can see the sky and the stars. Sukkots go back to biblical times. For the Jews, they represent memories of their wandering through the desert protected by clouds of glory.

My grandmother was the oldest of nine. They lived in a lovely home that my great-grandfather had built. Her best friend built the house next door, and it was a mirror image of my great-grandfather Isaac's home! Every fall, when it was time for Sukkot, an eight-day festival, my great-grandfather would roll back a tin ceiling that was attached to a pulley system in the kitchen. Once that was rolled back, branches were laid across the open space, and the children would hang vegetables and fruits from the branches. And so, their Sukkah was created.

For my grandmother, it was a happy time, a week filled with treats and special delicious foods, like honey and apples, and sharing her father's lap with one or two other children. She always looked happy when she talked about her Sukkah.

I grew up in the modem era. My parents moved away from these traditions, and I hadn't even had the experience of walking into a Sukkah. However, there was something powerful and magnetic about my grandmother's memories. In a sense, they were transferred to me as beacons of light of things I had yet to experience.

For many years, our neighbors and our family built a little Sukkah. It had three sides with an open roof. The boys went across to the lake and found bamboo branches, and we strung them up and hung decorations. We've had friends over, as well as my parents, and we sat outside in the mellow autumn evenings. One day, as the Sukkot was drawing to a close, I sat alone having a cup of coffee in the Sukkah. The weather was glorious, and everything around me seemed to be in perfect harmony. I felt so close to my grandmother and her memories. Her positive memories had finally come to fruition. I thought, "Look Grandma, I'm really sitting in a Sukkah!"

It's important to realize that we have access to many positive memories, not only those that we ourselves have experienced.

Our minds are magical and can take the happiness and stories of others and build from them if we give ourselves half a chance.

Take a few moments and, instead of perhaps feeling sad or disappointed for something you never got to experience in your life, think about a wonderful experience that someone else told you about. See if you can let their positive memories find a home in your memory bank.

Happy sharing of positive memories!

Chapter Fifty-Four

NEW YEAR'S RESOLUTIONS

My wish for you on New Year's Eve is that the one resolution you will really keep this year, even more than your diet, is to be true to yourself. And if you have a daughter, help and encourage her to be true to herself. I wrote *The Truth: I'm Ten, I'm Smart and I Know Everything* to help girls and their moms avoid getting caught in social and emotional vices that have plagued women for centuries. It is easy for us to lose some of the best of ourselves. We always have to be vigilant. We give so much of ourselves, but not always do we give enough to ourselves. The biggest gift that a ten-year-old can receive from you is the sense that she is amazing. She is gifted, smart, funny, wise, inventive, capable and simply wonderful. And the biggest gift you can give yourself is permission to get back to the energy inside yourself that is just as marvelous. You will find yourself living out a true recipe for happiness.

May you and your daughter(s) be blessed in the New Year by truly seeing and loving the best in yourselves.

Chapter Fifty-Five

OUR SPECIAL ANGELS

In the Jewish tradition, we talk a lot about Elijah. He is a very special angel who has all sorts of mystical duties. It is traditional to leave a glass of wine for Elijah at our Passover Table and to open the door for Elijah so he can enter and drink along with all the rest of us. He is so important that he is everyone's guest! People long to see him, and there is a tradition that once in a while he comes to earth in earthly form. Sometimes he is a beggar. This type of appearance reminds us to never ignore the needy. And other times he is in other forms.

Here is a story about Elijah that is meaningful to all of us loosely based on a rabbi's* talk.

Once there was a man who wanted so very much to meet the angel Elijah that he prayed day and night for this uplifting meeting. If only it could take place! So, he decided to go to a great rabbi and ask his advice on how he could meet up with Elijah.

The rabbi pondered this man's request for a long time and finally answered:

"This is what you should do. There is a poor widowed woman who lives at the edge of town with many children. They have hardly enough to eat and dress in rags. Go to them the day before Rosh Hashanah and bring them lots of healthy, delicious food. And also bring them clothes and other household goods you can think of. This should help you to see Elijah."

The man was thrilled. He joyfully asked his wife to prepare extra food for the holiday. He eagerly put together bags of his family's used clothes and even asked neighbors for used household goods and more clothing. His wagon was full by the time he arrived at the run-down cottage at the edge of town where the woman and her children lived.

The children came out to greet him. Soon, they were dancing and laughing with glee as the wagon was unloaded. Their mother stood in shock, not able to move. Finally, she said, "Thank you, you have saved us!"

The man went home happy and uplifted, but later became sad, as he realized he had not met Elijah.

So, after Rosh Hashanah, he went back to the rabbi and told him what he had done and of his distress at still not seeing Elijah.

This time the rabbi took even longer to answer. Finally, he said, "Go back again to the same woman's house. It is the day before Yom Kipper, and they need food again. This time you will see Elijah."

The man left, a little disgruntled. Maybe the rabbi should have suggested a different family. Or even going to a strange town. He had already gone there, and nothing happened. Still, he got his wife to help him and soon his wagon was full of delicious food and treats.

As he came up to the cottage, no one came to greet him. He heard crying through the open window. He drew his horse to a halt and listened.

Inside a boy was crying, "How can I fast tomorrow? We have no food today. I'm supposed to eat a lot today, to have the strength to fast tomorrow! I can't do this!"

And soon another child, a teenage girl, was heard sobbing. "And how will you fast, Mommy. You will be so weak!"

And the mother then replied, "I don't know. But I do know that we have to fast. Maybe there will be a miracle like last week.

We were hungry then, too, and our clothes were in rags. And remember, the angel Elijah came and saved us! So, don't give up, it is still early in the day and plenty of time to eat for tomorrow!"

The man was awestruck. The woman had called him Elijah! Soon, he knocked on the door and cries of elation broke out. The kids called him "Elijah" as the food was unloaded. He was hugged and kissed, and the family called out his *name* and thanked him as he and his horse left to return home.

Surprise and happiness filled his heart. What did this mean? Surely, he was not an angel!

And that is where the rabbi left the story, going on to say, that we can all become Elijahs. All we have to do is look around and take positive action and do good deeds when they are necessary. Elijah may be an angel, but he is also on earth every day, potentially in every person.

*The story was told by Rabbi Lichenstein of Lakewood. I heard it second hand, so I apologize if I left out important details. I hope I caught and transmitted the essence.

Chapter Fifty-Six

HAVING FUN

My dear friend and mentor, Mr. Del Sylvester, used to say that if you become interested in anything, it will become interesting. I knew Mr. Sylvester when I was a teenager. I don't think I fully understood this concept then. Now, I do. I see that if we bother to get interested in an activity or in somebody, most of the time, that activity or person becomes more and more interesting to us. For example, if I start to knit, I may get a kick out of the first line of stitches. But if I hang in, and I'm wearing a beautiful sweater that I knitted, I am sure to get even more pleasure from this new hobby. Likewise, if you adopt a pet, you are often amazed at how special he is as you get to play with him. Suddenly, you are in love!

Here is a way to get your mind stimulated. What are three activities you would like to get interested in? In fact, to make it even more interesting, what are three things or activities you would like to do for a week? Here are three I would enjoy:

1. Studying about unsolved mysteries of the world and universe with great thinkers and scientists.

2. Learning about gourmet foods, and beverages of the world with top culinary experts, with hands on cooking events.

3. Working with a prop professional on a movie set and learning how to find accurate props to recreate the 1940s.

Now, what would you like to spend a week getting interested in?

Chapter Fifty-Seven

FINDING A TREASURE CHEST

Have you ever wished for the Publishers Clearing House to come to your door one bright and early morning? Or perhaps you bought a lottery ticket, feeling the anticipation of being sent a substantial check every week for the rest of your life? Although you may not realize it, metaphorically the Publishers Clearing House comes by your door every morning, and every day you have the winning lottery ticket. How is this possible? Well, within you, there already exists a treasure chest. It is filled with the priceless jewels of your own positive memories and your capacities to achieve positive states of being.

Don't be afraid to open up that treasure chest and peek inside. Ah! What is that first jewel, that shiny object that resembles a beautiful sparkling sapphire? That jewel represents something positive that happened to you. What was it? Was it those few minutes you sat on the porch and watched the sun's rays shining through the trees? Or was it when a friend called and invited you to come over — perhaps the friend that you had meant to call many months ago but didn't call? Or was it nothing in particular other than all the breaths of air that you inhaled and exhaled or the heart beats that continue to support the being that is you?

You'll have to decide what that sapphire really is, as well as the diamond and the ruby and all those beautiful pearls. Each one belongs to you, and each one is a positive memory that you can tap into again and again.

Down in that treasure chest also lurks some of your lost potential from childhood, the things you could have done, the ways you could have developed if only things had been different. Those are the ones that need to be rubbed and polished. They look dingy at the bottom of the treasure chest. Take them out and buff them with a cloth. Then you can begin to see how you can reinvent yourself. It may be too late to become an Olympic athlete, or a movie star, or even the president of the United States, but it isn't too late to get that body in shape, lift some weights, or ride a bicycle. It's not too late to get active in local politics, join a theatrical group, or rent some fine old movies.

Maybe you will have to hold up some of those jewels to the light and look at them from different angles. Finding what is precious about ourselves takes time and effort. We don't always see at first glance how we can reintegrate and develop our strengths, talents, and lost potential into a person who is able to achieve positive states of being again and again.

Recognizing that your own treasure chest of positive memories and capacities are more precious to you than any winnings is what THE ENCHANTED SELF is all about.

When we begin to acknowledge that we ourselves are our own messengers of enchantment, then we can begin to brighten our lives and the lives around us.

Chapter Fifty-Eight

DESIGNING YOUR LIFE

As we pass through the Seven Gateways to Enchantment again and again, and become a true Enchanted Self, we see that life is all about living and then telling and retelling the stories of our lives to get the most positive juice from our stories.

This often means taking pain and misfortune and turning it into meaning and eventually a metamorphosis of pleasure. One example of designing a fulfilling life comes to mind. This is the story of a part of our French cousin's life. A retired doctor living outside of Paris, Jean Manuel, has often told us the story of his years living hidden in a farmhouse in a French province. When he was five, his parents were warned that they had to leave Paris. He vividly remembers how terribly upset his parents were. Somehow, they found a farmer and his wife who agreed to take in as many of the family members as could get there. His family and some cousins lived for several years on this farm.

Others chose not to leave Paris and were never heard of again.

Jean Manuel told us how his family went back after the war to look for their missing relatives, only to find possessions and an uneaten birthday cake celebrating the nephew's first birthday still on the table at one of their cousin's homes. The family, however, was gone forever. He remembers his parents' despair, yet also how life resumed for all of them.

He also shared with us how his father was once picked up by the French Police and loaded onto a train. Fortunately, the train was moving slowly enough that his father could jump and escape, living for a while in the woods until he could return to his family.

One might at first wonder how a person could come to terms with so much loss and seeing his family go through so much pain. I don't know Jean Manuel terribly well, but I have clearly seen a friendly, joyful person every time we've been together. I have a hunch of ways he has processed this story of his life and the life of his family.

I believe that one of the major ways that he has processed his own life and turned it into a meaningful, joyful experience is by giving back. The farmer and his wife who took them in didn't have any children of their own. Jean Manuel and everyone else that was hidden by them never forgot them. They visited this couple every summer. To this very day, although the husband is gone, and the wife lives in a nursing home, Jean Manuel or his wife or his daughter will take the responsibility of visiting and being with this woman. They never forget, and they've always been good to the people that were good to them.

Perhaps the other major way that I know that this man had made his life story into a meaningful life adventure is the way I feel when I am with him. He is a pleasant, reassuring person who makes me feel comfortable, safe, and as if there is a good time lurking around every corner. I think he is a lovely example of someone living an enchanted life... a life that has had to be reinterpreted, I'm sure, more than once... a life that is not a life of fame but of meaning and consistency.

Exercise: Positive Personal Recognition

The following activity is great to help you better recognize how special you really are. Keep a piece of paper or a small notebook handy with which to make a self-pride list. For one week, write down at least one item a day that you have done well.

For example, on your list you might put, "I was polite and kind to several people in the check-out line in the supermarket, even though I was very tired." Or you might write, "I used my head, rather than my fists," or "Today I was able to really share with my son my concerns over his getting another traffic ticket, rather than showing intense anger." Or you might write something as simple as, "I took care of my body today. I ate reasonable foods and went for a 20-minute walk."

At the end of the week, find a spare moment to read over your list a few times. After you have done that, give yourself a mental hug or visualize shaking hands with yourself or giving yourself a high five or even placing a gold star on your forehead. This is a good way to give yourself some recognition and possibly long overdue acknowledgment of all your many successes.

What you will realize as you keep your list is that you are certainly worth acknowledging in positive ways! You may also be surprised to see that you have done many acts of kindness, good deeds, and taken positive rather than negative action! Wow, you are an ENCHANTED SELF!

Chapter Fifty-Nine

FINDING MAGIC POTIONS

When I talk about magic potions — an expression I use to add drama and fire to our cold winter days — I am really talking about individual mental health formulas designed for each person. These are available in various sizes, shapes, and compositions. Just like the old-fashioned pharmacy where the pharmacist got out his mortar and pestle and mixed a compound for you when you didn't feel well, our mental health magic potions are that unique, requiring individual mixing. In fact, a compound that agrees with me may not agree with you. So, it is very important to take the time to mix exactly what each of us need. This is necessary for the full effect of joy and rejuvenation that each of us deserve each holiday season.

Now, let's look at what makes a mental health potion real magic. The best way I can teach you about these magic potions is by example. For me, a magic potion this time of year is simply to walk outside the house, as I did one morning, to listen to a crow up in a tree calling its song. This ordinary bird, not usually sought after for its song, has always quickened my heart and unleashed a momentary but real sense of well-being.

For many years I've wondered why. The best I can determine is that I have memories, partially forgotten, which I call "shadow prints of the mind" in my book, *The Enchanted Self: A Positive Therapy*.

These vague memories are without a clear storyline but seem to take me back to my grandmother Rose Silverman that I loved so much. The crow's call starts a memory trace that includes Rosen Road where my grandparents lived. I do not remember any crows calling, but I do remember lying in my bed and experiencing the wider world through an open window.

I felt content lying there, enjoying the aromas of flowers and cooking, the street noises, including children's voices laughing and shouting, cars and, of course, nature's voice: the birds chirping and the trees rustling. All of this made me feel so safe, drowsily content, and anticipating what our adventures that day would be.

Perhaps I'd get to ride on the swan boats downtown at Boston Common, feed the pigeons, and grandpa would buy me a balloon. Or maybe we would be going to visit a relative, and I would be offered a wonderful box of chocolates from which to pick one or two special selections. Then I would get to dance and show off and receive some well appreciated praise.

How lovely to bring all that back in a flash! I want to thank the crow that was up in the tree that day for being there and so exquisitely offering me the exact mental health potion that I needed to start my day.

Chapter Sixty

CHILDREN AND SELF ESTEEM

Anyone raising a child realizes how exhausting and difficult it can be to be a parent. At every stage of development there are problems: how to potty-train, separation anxiety, starting school, nightmares, siblings fighting, poor eating habits, whining, loss of a pet, getting adjusted to a new school, bullying, friend drama, etc.

But perhaps nothing equals the anxiety, rage, and panic a parent can have once her child reaches the tween and teen years. Looming in front of her are all the reports on drugs, drinking, overdoses, suicides, guns, and constant social media. YIKES!

Parties, friends, learning to drive, drinking, bullying, schoolwork, family fighting, crushes, and too early sexual activity. How can we stay alert to tween and teen danger?

1. It's never too late to sit down with your tween and teen and go over the rules of your home. That can include among your

unique rules such as shoes off at the front door, more general rules such as curfew hours, chores, cell phone usage, keeping you up to date on where they are, money constraints, etc.

2. Rules are great, but you don't have to stop with the formality of the do's and don'ts. It is a perfect time to talk about values and issues. Tell your tween or teen what your values are around such things as alcohol, drugs, sex, vulgar language, etc. Don't be afraid. They want to know what you think about serious matters. And make sure you are clear about what is legal in your state. If the drinking age is 21, or even 18, if she is 17 and invited to have a beer at someone's home, there is only one clear answer. "No, thank you."

3. Most important, is to help your tween or teen understand that you are on their side. No matter what tight spot they may find themselves in, they can always call upon you for help and guidance. Yes, you may be angry and at times even have to "act like a parent" and yell or insist on things going a certain way, but it all comes from love and having taken on the responsibility of helping your child grow up to be a wonderful adult.

Take a look at the film clip above from *Help from Beyond, A Coming of Age, Selfie Film*. I directed, wrote and am now creating the finished product. It spins off of my two books for girls, tweens and teens: *The Truth: Diary of a Gutsy Tween* and *Secrets: Diary of a Gutsy Teen*. In this scene, the girl has gone to a party where there is drinking. Her mother is furious, but also concerned. Can you relate to this scene? Feel free to share your thoughts.

Chapter Sixty-One

CREATING A MENTAL PLAYDATE

Time for a little homework, readers! Sometimes we are so busy thinking about working our bodies out or holding playdates with the kids, we forget one of the most important aspects of ourselves: our mental state. Sometimes, you just need to take a break and have a mental playdate. Stimulate your senses with this mind-blowing mental workout that can help reveal your inner potential. Relax, and let your mind drift backward in time. Give yourself permission to drift back to a younger age. Let your intuition be your guide in choosing an age. Once you have chosen, imagine yourself in a room in a childhood home. See the furniture and the colors of the room. Can you smell anything, any aromas of food cooking or other odors? Can you hear any noises or people talking? Is there a television on? What show might be on? Can you look out the window from where you're sitting? What do you see?

Take a couple of minutes to re-experience this childhood scene.

On a piece of paper, jot down all the positive thoughts and feelings you associate with this reflection. Then make a list of all the talents and positive capacities you had as a child at that age, whether they were recognized by anyone else in the world or just secretly and intuitively recognized by you.

Chapter Sixty-Two

KIDS HAVE DEEP THOUGHTS AND FEELINGS TOO

Kids worry all the time. Their thoughts, feelings, and emotions are as real and central to being alive as ours are. Mr. Fred Rogers knew that intimately and spent his entire television career helping kids know that they were special, and he liked them just the way they were. That message must never stop.

However, maybe often, in the hustle and bustle of living and getting kids ready for school, driving them to after-school activities, thinking about braces, homework, calling them out on minor offenses, worrying about how we will pay the bills, and sometimes much more serious dilemmas — someone is ill, dad lost his job, the marriage is falling apart, my kid is being bullied, there was another shooting in a public school, a cousin overdosed on drugs, etc. — we have no time to process the inner life of our kids.

But inner life exists and begs to be heard. Questions about how grown-ups handle serious issues such as school shootings bother kids on a daily basis. Perhaps your kid wonders how it is that Daddy and you go to work feeling safe in your offices, while kids who are unable to really care for themselves go to school in buildings where people can suddenly attack them and their teachers with automatic rifles.

Kids are deeply affected by how other kids are treated, even news items like kids being separated from parents at our borders can create feelings of despair, confusion, and worries about how we handle children in our country. Also, kids wonder how and why people end up seriously addicted or dead. And don't forget faith and religion, a topic older than that Bible. Kids wonder if there is an afterlife, why good people get hurt or killed, etc.

Let's not be blind sighted. We may not have all the answers to *deep* questions that have plagued sleepless nights of many for thousands of years, but we can be attentive to our children psychologically, spiritually, and even politically. Here are some suggestions:

Create time for your family to share good news, good deeds, disappointments, concerns, and questions. Creating a setting where people who love each other can sincerely listen and respond to anything from trivial good news to serious concerns will help your kids, whether they are 2 or 22, feel safer to share what is really on their minds. No putdowns, if possible, and your job is to truly listen and create this space. That means no phones on and maybe a treat, such as a favorite dessert. It also means you being honest and sharing your memories about *deep* thoughts and concerns and taking seriously what your kids bring up. Listening is only the first step. Action, where required, is the next.

For example, in this film clip: https://vimeo.com/275643285

The girl was very unsatisfied listening to her minister as he wasn't talking about the issues on her mind. Ideally, if she could have shared these feelings with her parents, they would try to come to some helpful conclusions. What they would decide is as unique as each family, but solutions could be to not force the girl to go to services right now, find a different church, discuss some of the *deep* issues of life at home, take social actions as a family in town, etc.

Beyond this film clip, if news events, from school shootings to overdoses to separation of kids from parents at border crossings upset or concern your kids, set a good example. Maybe call or write to your senators and congress people with your kids present. Maybe write a letter to the editor of your local paper with your kids giving some suggestions.

Chapter Sixty-Three

And finally

I hope you have enjoyed *Resilience and Self-esteem for Women*. I can't wait to hear from you. Please, if any of these stories or short essays opened your mind to a new way of looking at yourself, handling a member of your family, or making you feel more comfortable in daring to be you, please share by sending your writing to Barbara.Holstein@ gmail.com. You never know if what you discover and dare to write about yourself may help another woman somewhere live a more enchanted life of value and purpose. Sharing is a win-win for everyone. Of course, you will be notified if your story is chosen to be shared publicly in any way.

Chapter Sixty-Four

Building Resilience and Self-esteem: Interview with Moumita Basuroychowdhury, Part 1

I was recently interviewed by Moumita Basuroychowdhury. This is Part 1 of that interview.

Mental health has become a cornerstone of well-being in today's fast-paced world. It's not just about managing life's obstacles; it's about finding purpose, embracing happiness, and thriving despite challenges. Positive Psychology is a field of study that focuses on the strengths and virtues that enable individuals and communities to thrive. Dr. Barbara Becker Holstein, a true luminary in this holistic approach, has left an indelible mark on the field.

Dr. Barbara Becker Holstein's accomplishments as an author, filmmaker, and psychologist are a testament to her unwavering dedication to helping others find true happiness. Her innovative projects, spanning books, films, podcasts, and workbooks, have transformed countless lives, offering invaluable tools and insights for personal growth and self-discovery.

At the heart of Dr. Holstein's philosophy lies the transformative concept of THE ENCHANTED SELF. This powerful idea recognizes the unique energy force within each person, an enduring essence that, when nurtured and understood, can lead to profound personal transformation. THE ENCHANTED SELF is about harnessing and cultivating one's innate talents, strengths, and potential, empowering individuals to navigate their lives with resilience and joy.

Dr. Holstein's journey began in a quiet, contemplative space as an only child. Often finding herself alone, she sought friendships wherever she could. This solitude, however, became a fertile ground for her creativity and introspection, laying the foundation for her future work in Positive Psychology.

"I remember being very insistent on keeping a diary, which I started when I was nine. I dragged my mother to downtown Bridgeport, where we lived because I had to buy a diary. The only thing that felt appropriate was a Girl Scouts diary since I was in the Girl Scouts, and I kept it pretty faithfully for three or four years. I still have those little green books."

In those early diaries, she recorded the minutiae of daily life, such as what she ate for breakfast or how her mom made pancakes. "I wouldn't have dared to put anything really on my mind in the diary," she reflects, hinting at a more profound inner world that remained unspoken.

"Then, in my teenage days, I continued on loose-leaf paper with tons of diaries and poetry. By the time I was about 16, I had read a couple of psychology books that fell into my lap. I don't really remember how, but I was fascinated with the human mind."

Her love for conversation mirrored this fascination with the mind. She vividly recounts an instance at 16 when she traveled to Boston to visit her grandmother. "I talked to the lady next to me for two hours, even though we would likely never see each other again," she says, highlighting her innate curiosity about people.

Her parents, both educators, instilled in her a sense of possibility and encouraged her intellectual pursuits. An early memory from fourth grade stands out. She was tasked with giving a presentation to her class, a daunting prospect. Her father suggested she talk about "The Tortoise and the Hare," a story that subtly imparted the lesson of perseverance.

"He helped me a little bit, and I practiced the story. After speeding through part of the race, the hare lies down for a nap and gets nowhere. Moving slowly and steadily, the tortoise wins. The fascinating thing about this was my father was at the same time giving me a message: that I should just plow on, and I would make it."

Her mother, a schoolteacher, also played a crucial role in nurturing her curiosity. When she had to write a report on an insect, her mother suggested she pretend to be an ant and narrate life from an ant's perspective. This imaginative approach helped her engage more deeply with her studies, even as she struggled with dyslexia.

"I could not read anything and was already in the third grade. I had a severe disability, and in those days, nothing was picked up. You just made it, or you didn't. My teacher, Ms. Johnson, took me aside and said, 'Look, you're having trouble reading. I can tell. I want you to forget about sounding out words and memorize thousands of words. You can do it. Take your time, but you'll do it.'"

Her teacher's belief in her abilities led to a remarkable turnaround. By the end of the year, she was a top reader, surpassing her peers by several years in reading tests. This experience taught her the value of creative approaches to learning and instilled a lifelong belief in the power of perseverance.

Growing up with such inventive and compassionate role models, Dr. Holstein naturally gravitated towards intellectually engaging and artistic fields. She majored in philosophy at Barnard College, a subject that allowed her to delve into the depths of human thought and existence.

"That was close to the kind of deep thinking that goes with being a psychologist. It's just a little more skewed to other facets of how the mind works and what's real and what's not. My parents got me on the phone one day when I was a senior, and they said, 'So, okay, you majored in philosophy, and how are you going to support yourself?' I said, 'Well, I don't know. I want to be an actress. I want to be a lawyer. I love philosophy.'"

Recognizing the practicalities of life, her parents suggested she consider a career in teaching, given her love for people and working with kids. She took their advice, earning a master's degree in education from Boston University before ultimately receiving a fellowship and returning to earn a doctorate. It was during this time that she decided to focus on the human mind more generally rather than school psychology. "I realized that that's where I really wanted to go," she says.

Her initial interests in philosophy, poetry, and theater later blossomed into various avenues for healing, including workbooks, films, and novels. Her creative pursuits began to merge with her professional life, enriching her approach to therapy.

"My first poem woke me up during the night. It was somewhat deep and tied into a belief in God. I'm not sure where that came from, but I quickly found that all sorts of artistic things could relieve me in one way or another through the difficulties of growing up, and I experienced a lot of difficulties, as most of us do."

This ability to connect with the human condition helped her relate to both children and adults alike. Today, she applies this empathy in her practice in New Jersey, working with patients ranging from toddlers to adults.

"My patients vary from 2 years old to 92 years old. There are people who are depressed and anxious, kids and adults that need support or advice, perhaps recovering from a trauma, such as moving, or divorce or illness in the family and also people looking to explore their enchanted self."

Chapter Sixty-Five

Building Resilience and Self-esteem: Interview with Moumita Basuroychowdhury, Part 2

I was recently interviewed by Moumita Basuroychowdhury. This is Part 2 of that interview.

Dr. Barbara Becker Holstein has always felt that traditional psychology falls short of helping individuals reach self-actualization, instead focusing more on solving problems. She believes therapy sessions are usually too brief to delve deeply into a person's talents and hidden potential, which are crucial for long-term well-being.

"The problem is that the person's real talents and hidden potential that they may need to serve them the rest of their life are often overlooked or, at first glance, hidden. If people haven't been introduced and encouraged to use their talents, abilities and capacities, they're often not ready to move ahead. Maturing and living a long life requires the ability to move in and out of crises and disappointments and to get back on your horse because there's an energy inside you that's always there; it's your energy, it's your capacities, it's your insights and your potential for something that maybe your parents or life stifled, and now you're going to develop, that part of yourself that is enchanted, in that it is unique to you and can be replenished again and again."

This insight, which she gained decades ago, led to her developing the concept of THE ENCHANTED SELF, an idea that struck her while sitting by the ocean.

"That enchanted self is the part of you that is like an energy force. It never leaves, and maybe even goes on to the afterlife, I don't know. But it's always there. It must be trained, utilized and understood to be effective for you."

She began writing about this concept and was soon invited to speak at workshops, marking a turning point in her career.

"That was the turning point of turning from a very nice young lady therapist in her late 30s, doing a good job, to someone with unusual vision, a visionary."

Her work in Positive Psychology, particularly with women, gained traction. In 1996, she started a website where women could share their stories, pictures, and poetry. This online presence allowed her to reach a wider audience and foster a community of support and encouragement. This site, still very active, was one of the first sites on the web for women's wellness and creativity.

"It was and still is a beautiful, engaging, useful site. It went up at such a turning point in human relations — in 1996. At the time, most ordinary people did not have cell phones yet. You went to the library for information. It was just at the edge of all these changes. Looking back, I see it now as one of my visionary steps that I dared to take. A web home for women to share and learn and be productive before most women in the world even knew what the web was and certainly didn't know what place it would play in all of our lives. Women came in and out of my life who were helpful. And that site, it's still there."

Through a series of serendipitous encounters, her career marched forward. "I think you have to kind of recognize special moments," she says. One day, after training for the American Psychological Association, she was approached by a woman who told her about her TV show, which focused on the concept of goodness. The woman asked Dr. Holstein if she would like to be a guest on it.

"I almost fell in the street and got killed. I was like, oh, my God, I can't believe this. I was her guest a few times. Eventually,

I inherited the space once a month for THE ENCHANTED SELF show, and I did it for years."

The show featured various guests, including actors, cooks, authors, healers, yoga specialists, other psychologists, social workers, and authors. This exposure led to the creation of THE ENCHANTED SELF newsletter, which was immensely successful.

"Women were welcome to send in their stories and poetry. We always had a major topic in the front of the newsletter. My friend, Doreen Lapperton Addison, often worked with me. We did mind-body workshops and even a dance that she choreographed. We performed at Brookdale College, our local college. I got to be the enchantress who was leading the ladies and children to a land where they could be their greatest selves. It was a lovely 23-minute dance. Looking back, I realize I was teaching others about how to come home to their Enchanted Selves in many different ways and, at the same time, teaching myself."

Much of her work today focuses on women and girls, and she even has a channel on Roku called THE ENCHANTED SELF. She recognizes the unique challenges girls face today, particularly with the pervasive influence of social media and other modern temptations.

"I think in today's world, where there are drugs, social media, and easy access to a lot of stuff, young girls are tempted by many things. The temptation has always been there. I mean, I tried to smoke cigarettes when I was a teenager. I'd lock my bedroom door and sit on the bed. And I was just lucky because I had allergies, and I'd cough my way until I put the cigarette out."

"There has always been a pull towards imagination and the push of hormones growing up. In today's world, so much is apparent so easily. Often, girls don't know how to caution themselves because the world itself isn't helping that much in giving them a sense of how to handle hormonal development in their teenage years and how to handle falling in love or losing a best friend. How do you adequately handle these things so that girls don't become depressed?"

The pandemic exacerbated these challenges, isolating girls from their social networks and depriving them of significant milestones and opportunities for self-discovery.

"They're social and used to getting together with their friends all the time. They lost graduations, parties, seeing their best friends, and certain opportunities to discover themselves better."

Building Resilience and Self-esteem: Interview with Moumita Basuroychowdhury, Part 3

I was recently interviewed by Moumita Basuroychowdhury. This is Part 3 of that interview.

In response to recent societal shifts, Dr. Holstein has written workbooks, such as *Looking Good, Feeling Good*, for girls to help them navigate these turbulent times, often encouraging parents and family members to have meaningful conversations with them in the process.

"The way my books are set up, you can draw a picture, write a poem, and engage in discussions with your parents or family members. This involvement helps girls feel supported and understood."

She also encourages kids to create selfie films as a means of expressing themselves. This method allows them to articulate their feelings more comfortably and privately.

"You know, a lot of kids don't really want to talk with their parents. It's hard. But if you let them make a three-minute film on their phone and sit in a different room, very often, they can say, 'Look, I've been upset. I didn't know how to say it to you.' These workbooks and films are not just static like an old-fashioned workbook. They engage you in artistic ways to develop and share your wisdom. And that's become very important to me to help these girls, almost a lost generation, find their resiliency and self-esteem and learn how to hold on to it."

She emphasizes the critical nature of school years in shaping a person's life while acknowledging that it takes a village to support a child fully.

"Sometimes honesty is the best policy when it comes to parents sharing aspects of their lives. It gives kids a chance to feel they can come out of whatever they're doing that may not be the best for them. Parents often don't tell the kids enough about themselves."

She has written several books, including *The Truth: I'm Ten, I'm Smart, and I Know Everything*, which inspired two other books, *The Truth* and *Secrets*, which have been adapted into plays and films. These works explore the complexities of the human mind and the challenges of personal growth.

"My first book, *The Truth*, is a diary about a girl with at least 30 topics that really happened or could happen while growing up mentioned through her diary. It turned into two books, 'The Truth' and 'Secrets.' The diary format allows for a fuller development of character and background. The books also have space for the girl reading the book to keep diary notes that can remain private or be shared with her mother, family, etc.

I started to see certain scenes that would make very nice short film scenes, like how this girl felt when her parents were fighting and when she found out her father was taking a new job but hadn't told her. She heard it through the grandmother and the parents talking secretly behind closed doors, things like that, which often happen in real life."

She ultimately made a 16-minute film with the rest of her team. However, when they played it back, they felt something was missing. The editor suggested the actress go back and do all the scenes herself without the small crew watching.

"She moved to different rooms in her own house and out in the garden and walked in circles outside. We ended up with a magical 16 minutes, a film that is not only still playing at festivals but gave me the idea of selfie filmmaking, a way to bring aspects of drama to kids via their cell phones whenever appropriate — a way to be more in charge of whatever they want to be in charge of, whether it be making or acting in films to show at festivals or making a film to say what needed to be said to a parent that was too hard to say to the parent in person."

Dr. Holstein has adopted another visionary approach now that everyone has cell phones. She passionately encourages individuals of all ages to utilize their cell phones as a powerful tool to share, care, and nourish their mental health. She dreams of someday hosting a captivating show that unites children and experts from various fields to engage in meaningful conversations about improving mental well-being while addressing crucial aspects of growing up.

In the meantime, she has made available most of her coming-of-age selfie films for free on Vimeo so that teachers, parents, therapists, and kids can view these award-winning films. "Why wait? Kids, parents, teachers, and clinicians need the films now," she says. Her curated showcase on Vimeo features these dramatic selfie films that offer valuable insights into the challenges of growing up, providing much-needed support for parents and children.

Then she wrote a third book, *Conflict and a Bit of Magic*, which follows the main character from the first two books, *The Truth* and *Secrets*, as she ages. "The series can help a kid and her parents get through some of those difficult times. Best to read them together if possible or at least share some pages," she says. Dr. Holstein has also written several books geared towards adults, such as *The Enchanted Self: A Positive Therapy* and *Recipes for Enchantment: The Secret Ingredient is YOU!* With the help of producer Debbie Higgens, she also created Zoom dramas during the pandemic, adapting her scripts for virtual performances. This innovative approach allowed her to continue her work despite the limitations imposed by the pandemic.

"We did 'Life is Complicated,' a Zoom drama. It's a dramatic adaptation of a script, and it has won awards in film festivals. These experimental films have been accepted because the world has expanded, and there is now a place for mobile filmmaking and experimental filmmaking."

She likes to envision them as the extended drama of the main character in her books if she were older.

"It could be if she, another four or five years older, got married, and there were problems. They're trying to have a baby. They're not always nice to each other. There's a dream sequence where her earlier self comes back and helps her pull herself together, which is one of the things that I believe. We go back to our early energies, and they roll into helping us get out of whatever mess we're in this time."

She continued to create three or four more dramas based on either books she had written or subject matter that came to her. In addition, Dr. Holstein has a podcast where she invites guests such as educators, parents, young people, environmental specialists and people from various fields to speak about their experiences. She also has a new podcast geared to helping girls. Some topics covered include resilience and self-esteem. She is actively looking for guests to do projects in these areas.

Dr. Holstein's dedication to Positive Psychology and creative expression continues to inspire her work. She believes tapping into our energies and acknowledging our talents can lead to profound personal growth and healing.

"I think we shy away from improving ourselves because its human nature — it's tiring and a little embarrassing to recognize certain things, even if it's just to ourselves. But if you can have one episode where you recognize that your own energy saved the day, you're more likely to be willing to play with that again and again."

Her work as a positive psychologist and an author underscores the importance of Positive Psychology in fostering resilience and self-esteem. She hopes to continue writing and creating, helping others discover their enchanted selves.

"I do believe that *The Enchanted Self: A Positive Therapy* is a great book. It's my masterpiece. It has exercises at the end of the chapters to help you connect with your talents and strengths.

It's about recapturing your own energies and getting rid of the garbage that hinders the flow of your own energy."

She is now writing two new novels. One of the books is called *The Girls Down the Hall*, while the second is still untitled.

"They are about young women from the 1960s, which is actually when I started college. The reason I'm writing them is tied into so much stuff with abortion and all these issues turning on their heads for women. I don't really talk about that directly, but I tell the story of these girls from their freshman year, and then, hopefully, I'll continue each book as a series as they go through college. They show the complexity of women's minds, the issues they face, the disappointments they meet, and that it was tough then, and it's still very hard now, often for women to reach their full potential. But these are novels, and they're interesting, and they're fun. I am very enthused with them."

Dr. Holstein's journey is a testament to the power of creativity, perseverance, and the human spirit. Her work has touched many lives, helping people of all ages find their path to self-discovery and healing.

"For most people, we get caught in the belief system and the attitudes we got growing up, and we need to be shaken up a little to get to broader reactions and possibilities."